GRAMMAR MATTERS

Sentence Basics and Essential Grammar

GRAMMAR MATTERS

Sentence Basics and Essential Grammar

Anthony C. Winkler

Jo Ray McCuen-Metherell
Glendale Community College

Prentice Hall

Boston   Columbus   Indianapolis   New York   San Francisco   Upper Saddle River
Amsterdam   Cape Town   Dubai   London   Madrid   Milan   Munich   Paris   Montréal
Toronto Delhi   Mexico City   São Paulo   Sydney   Hong Kong   Seoul   Singapore   Taipei   Tokyo

Editor-in-Chief: Eric Stano
Senior Acquisitions Editor: Matthew Wright
Editorial Assistant: Samantha Neary
Senior Marketing Manager: Thomas DeMarco
Project Manager: Anne Ricigliano
**Project Coordination, Text Design, and Electronic
   Page Makeup:** Integra
Cover Design Manager: Leslie Osher
Cover Designer: Ximena Tamvakopoulos
Cover Photo: istockphoto
Manufacturing Buyer: Mary Ann Gloriande
Printer and Binder: Edwards Brothers
Cover Printer: Lehigh-Phoenix Color/Hagerstown

Library of Congress Cataloging-in-Publication Data

Winkler, Anthony C.
   Grammar matters: sentence basics and essential grammar/Anthony C. Winkler,
Jo Ray McCuen-Metherell. — 1st ed.
      p. cm.
Includes bibliographical references and index.
ISBN 978-0-205-05705-4 (alk. paper)
1. English language—Sentences.   2. English language—Grammar.   I. McCuen,
Jo Ray, 1929-   II. Title.
PE1441.W556 2011
428.2—dc22

                                                              2010050168

1 2 3 4 5 6 7 8 9 10—EDW—14 13 12 11

Prentice Hall
is an imprint of

www.pearsonhighered.com

ISBN-13: 978-0-205-05705-4
ISBN-10:   0-205-05705-5

CONTENTS

PEARSON
mywritinglab

If practice makes perfect, imagine what *better* practice can do . . .

MyWritingLab is an online learning system that provides better writing practice through progressive exercises. These exercises move students from literal comprehension to critical application to demonstration of their ability to write properly. With this better practice model, students develop the skills needed to become better writers!

When asked if they agreed with the following statements, students responded favorably.

97%
The MyWritingLab Student-user Satisfaction Level

"MyWritingLab helped me to improve my writing." 89%

"MyWritingLab was fairly easy to use." 90%

"MyWritingLab helped make me feel more confident about my writing ability." 83%

"MyWritingLab helped me to better prepare for my next writing course." 86%

"MyWritingLab helped me get a better grade." 82%

"I wish I had a program like MyWritingLab in some of my other courses." 78%

"I would recommend my instructor continue using MyWritingLab." 85%

Student Success Story

"The first few weeks of my English class, my grades were at approximately 78%. Then I was introduced to MyWritingLab. I couldn't believe the increase in my test scores. My test scores had jumped from that low score of 78 all the way up to 100% (and every now and then a 99)."
—Exetta Windfield, *College of the Sequoias* (MyWritingLab student user)

If your book did not come with an access code, you may purchase an access code at www.mywritinglab.com

PEARSON
mywritinglab™

Registering for MyWritingLab™…

*It is easy to get started! Simply follow these steps to get into your
MyWritingLab course.*

1) **Find Your Access Code** (it is either packaged with your textbook, or you purchased
   it separately). You will need this access code and your course ID to join your
   MyWritingLab course. Your instructor has your course ID number, so make sure
   you have that before logging in.

2) **Click on "Students"** under "Register or Buy Access." Here you will be prompted to
   enter your access code, enter your e-mail address, and choose your own login name and
   password. After you register, you can **login under "Returning Users"** to use your new
   login name and password every time you go back into MyWritingLab.

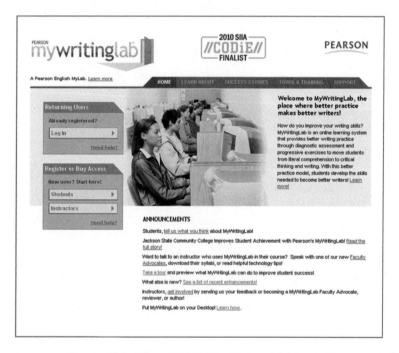

After logging in, you will see all the ways MyWritingLab can help you become a better writer.

PEARSON
mywritinglab

The Homepage ...

Here is your MyWritingLab HomePage.
You get a bird's eye view of where you are in your course every time you log in.

Your **Course** box shows your class details.

Your **Study Plan** box shows what you last completed and what is next on your **To Do** list.

Your **Gradebook** box shows you a snapshot of how you are doing in the class.

Your **Other Resources** box supplies you with amazing tools such as:

- **Pearson Tutor Services**—click here to see how you can get help on your papers by qualified tutors . . . before handing them in!

- **Research Navigator**—click here to see how this resembles your library with access to online journals for research paper assignments.

- **Study Skills**—extra help that includes tips and quizzes on how to improve your study skills

Now, let's start practicing to become better writers. Click on the Study Plan tab. This is where you will do all your course work.

The Study Plan ...

MyWritingLab provides you with a simple Study Plan of the writing skills that you need to master. You start from the top of the list and work your way down. You can start with the Diagnostic Pre-Tests.

The Diagnostic Pre-Tests contain five exercises on each of the grammar, punctuation, and usage topics. You can achieve mastery of the topic in the Diagnostic Pre-Test by getting four of five or five of five correct within each topic.

After completing the Diagnostic Pre-Test, you can return to your Study Plan and enter any of the topics you have yet to master.

Watch, Recall, Apply, Write . . .

Here is an example of a MyWritinglab Activity set that you will see once you enter into a topic. Take the time to briefly read the introductory paragraph, and then watch the engaging video clip by clicking on "Watch: Tense."

The video clip provides you with a helpful review.
Now you are ready to start the exercises. There are three types:

- Recall—activities that help you *recall* the rules of grammar

- Apply—activities that help you *apply* these rules to brief paragraphs or essays

- Write—activities that ask you to demonstrate these rules of grammar in your own writing

Helping Students Succeed ...

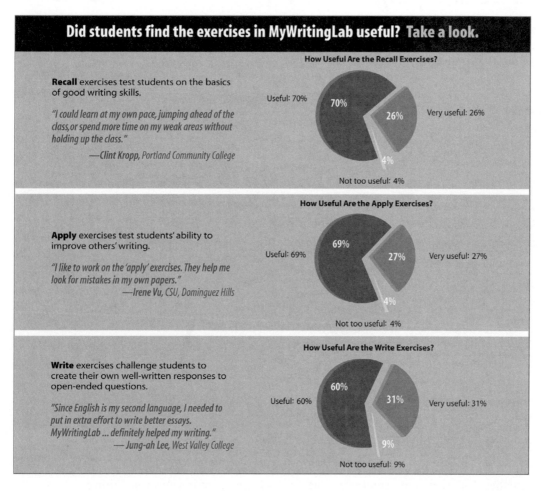

Did students find the exercises in MyWritingLab useful? Take a look.

Recall exercises test students on the basics of good writing skills.

"I could learn at my own pace, jumping ahead of the class, or spend more time on my weak areas without holding up the class."

—*Clint Kropp, Portland Community College*

How Useful Are the Recall Exercises?

Useful: 70%   70%   26%   Very useful: 26%

4%

Not too useful: 4%

Apply exercises test students' ability to improve others' writing.

"I like to work on the 'apply' exercises. They help me look for mistakes in my own papers."

—*Irene Vu, CSU, Dominguez Hills*

How Useful Are the Apply Exercises?

Useful: 69%   69%   27%   Very useful: 27%

4%

Not too useful: 4%

Write exercises challenge students to create their own well-written responses to open-ended questions.

"Since English is my second language, I needed to put in extra effort to write better essays. MyWritingLab ... definitely helped my writing."

— *Jung-ah Lee, West Valley College*

How Useful Are the Write Exercises?

Useful: 60%   60%   31%   Very useful: 31%

9%

Not too useful: 9%

Students just like you are finding MyWritingLab's Recall, Apply, and Write exercises useful in their learning.

PEARSON
mywritinglab™

Here to Help You ...

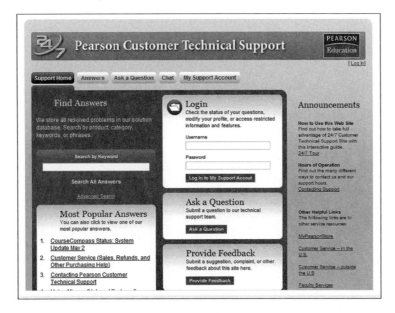

Our goal is to provide answers to your MyWritingLab questions as quickly as possible and deliver the highest level of support. By visiting **www.mywritinglab.com/help.html**, many questions can be resolved in just a few minutes. Here you will find help on the following:

☑ System Requirements

☑ How to Register for MyWritingLab

☑ How to Use MyWritingLab

For student support, we also invite you to contact Pearson Customer Technical Support (shown above). In addition, you can reach our Support Representatives online at **http://247.pearsoned.com**. Here you can do the following:

☑ Search Frequently Asked Questions about MyWritingLab

☑ E-mail a Question to Our Support Team

☑ Chat with a Support Representative

PREFACE

The essence of writing grammatically is writing appropriately. Writing that is grammatical is always appropriate in its language; writing that is not appropriate to the occasion or the audience is likely to be regarded as ungrammatical. How appropriateness is judged is based on usage. Take, for example, the use of "ain't" in place of the more conventional "aren't." Most English teachers would mark such use as bad grammar. Linguists classify *ain't* as one of several contractions of auxiliary verbs and trace its evolution from *amn't* through *an't* to its first recorded use in 1695, when it locked horns with a newer form emerging into popular use—*aren't.* After that, it was downhill for poor *ain't.* By the 19th century, *ain't* had been demoted to the rank of a *vulgarism,* meaning a word suitable for use only by the lower classes. Today, except for humorous usage, *ain't* has been forever banished from formal discourse.

Tireless memorization is one of the few certain ways to master English grammar if you have no relative in the field of law whose usage you can emulate. Drills and practices can help you remember odd irregularities. People prefer the language they hear spoken around them from birth. An English infant reared in a genteel drawing room will emerge from childhood speaking like an Englishman or Englishwoman reared in a genteel drawing room. He or she will avoid saying *ain't* to anyone but the hired help. Transplant that same infant to Brooklyn, and he or she will grow up speaking like someone brought up in Brooklyn. We have never seen an exception to this observation. Thus, we learn to speak our mother tongue not from a book, but from using our ears.

But what if you were born in the kitchen, as most of our ancestors were, and not in the palace rooms? You'd grow up speaking like the kitchen help. Our point is that to learn grammar properly, you'd have to steep yourself in the usage of the public vocabulary—which means hovering within earshot of the queen and the king so that you could copy the way they talk. Lacking that opportunity, you'd have to take a class that uses this book.

This book is grounded in the practical realities of acceptable usage and therefore of good grammar. You can find within these pages virtually everything you want to know in order to write grammatically. In down-to-earth, no-nonsense language, we begin with the basic sentence as seen from the viewpoints of native speakers and ESL students, and then move briskly to the 20 most common sentence errors and how to correct them. Every idea is followed by drills and practices galore to make sure you understand the point.

There are occasions when, no matter the background of the student, the ear and habit are at odds with the formal rule and are of no help whatsoever in deciding what is right and appropriate. A case in point is the infamous *between you and I.* Although used by a surprising array of prominent men and women in the media, this construction is technically incorrect. Yet, the correct form, *between you and me,* often sounds wrong. In this book, we occasionally draw special attention to these kinds of common "ear delinquencies." Moreover, to add some spice to the otherwise bland explanations of grammatical rules, we have included two humorous features:

- First are several cartoons that allow you to laugh at grammar while studying the rules.

- Second is a shrewd little icon called "Usage Monitor" that flags some bad habits you might need to get rid of. This distinctive character warns you of points of grammar on which the ear and habit cannot be trusted.

Our thanks to Matthew Wright, Senior Acquisitions Editor at Pearson, who proposed this book and oversaw its publication, and to the editing and manufacturing staff who helped with the multitude of details involved in seeing this book roll off the press, including Anne Ricigliano of Pearson and Debbie Meyer of Integra.

Anthony C. Winkler
Jo Ray McCuen-Metherell

SENTENCE BASICS

Part One of this book begins by explaining why grammar matters and why it is crucial to your career to master its principles. Then it moves on to a discussion of the differences between native born students and those who have learned English as a second language. However, Part One concentrates on the sentence. Bear in mind that most of the time when you string words together, you end up creating a sentence, and that is as it should be. The sentence is the heart of all writing, its source and foundation. But every sentence, no matter how short, reveals good or bad grammar. "Pete and **me was** pretending to be cool cats" is bad grammar whereas "Pete and **I were** pretending to be cool cats" is good grammar—a difference this book will teach you.

In observing our students, we have encountered two attitudes toward writing: The first is to see writing as fun, with sentences emerging as a spontaneous expression of one's personality. The second is to see writing as a hard and lonely task, where sentences are formed with difficulty. In the first approach, the writer has an idea, and then the words come tumbling after without thought of rewriting or second-guessing. The student clicks away at the computer, and the words effortlessly turn into sentences. In the second approach, the act of writing is agonizing because forming each sentence is like pushing a heavy wheelbarrow uphill. The student labors under the burden of what to write.

We conclude that methods of writing differ from writer to writer, and we tell our students that whichever method helps them transfer to paper what they have in their minds is the right method for them. Regardless of whether writing comes easy or hard for you, in the end, your goal should be to use the English language with as much power and as little clutter as possible—and with correct grammar.

In the hands of the right person, sentences can become immortal. For instance, the following sentences have survived over the decades because they are sleek, sharp, and grammatically correct:

A lie can travel half way around the world while truth is putting on its shoes.

—Mark Twain

As I would not be a slave, so I would not be a master. This is my idea of democracy.

—Abraham Lincoln

A house is not a home.

—Polly Adler

Take away love, and earth is a tomb.

—Robert Browning

Pay attention to this part of the book so that you will craft strong sentences that corroborate that grammar matters.

1 GRAMMAR MATTERS

Learning Objectives

- Learn the difference between prescriptive and descriptive grammar

- Understand why grammar really does matter

- Explain and understand a brief history of grammar

What is the point of studying grammar if you can understand speech and writing that is ungrammatical? That is a fair question and one many students quietly ask themselves if they do not outright ask their instructor. Some lyrics of popular songs deliberately make grammatical errors for the sake of a catchy rhyme. Take, as an example, the following lyrics from a megahit by Roger Miller:

> England swings like a pendulum do
>
> Bobbies on bicycles, two by two
>
> Westminster Abbey, the tower of Big Ben
>
> The rosy red cheeks of the little children*

Do you see the grammatical error? It is an error of agreement that pairs a singular subject, "pendulum," with a plural verb, "do." But if the writer had

---

* "England Swings" © 1965 Sony/ATV Music Publishing LLC. All rights administered by Sony/ATV Music Publishing LLC, 8 Music Square West, Nashville, TN 37203. All rights reserved. Used by permission.

chosen grammatical correctness over a catchy rhyme and written "a pendulum does," preserving the principle of agreement might have come at the expense of a hit song.

There are many other examples in popular culture of a lyricist choosing to sacrifice grammar to achieve popularity. A conspicuous example is the Elvis Presley monster hit "Hound Dog," which commits the mother of all deadly sins—using the ungrammatical *ain't* in place of *aren't*, as in, "You ain't nothin' but a hound dog." The truth is that "you're nothin' but a hound dog" just doesn't cut it in the overheated slang of the streets. Yet, to the ear of the grammarian, using *ain't* instead of *aren't* is as close to a capital offense as you can get. What's going on here?

In an ideal world, grammar would be nothing more than a universal system of road signs that every user must follow. The system would have no prejudice for or against the use of one word over another; we would have a clear idea of how punctuation marks should be used; and everyone who uses language would go skipping down the yellow brick road with no fear of falling into disrepute because of accidental bad usage.

Unfortunately, such a system, if it exists, is beyond the reach of our science and technology. The best we can offer today's writers is an explanation of two modern approaches to grammar. They are *prescriptive* grammar and *descriptive* grammar, and in influence and practice, they define the North and South Poles of grammatical theory.

Prescriptive grammar is grammar that is looked at medicinally. The prescriptive grammarian believes that the rules of grammar cure bad communication and are absolute. Grammatical teachings do not vary with local usage and custom, and a mistake made in one conversational context is the same as a mistake made in another. Grammar is grammar, as universal and firm as the law of gravity. And *ain't* is always wrong.

The descriptive grammarian believes quite the opposite—namely, that grammar varies with custom and usage. If the people living in a valley all regularly use "ain't" instead of "aren't," then "ain't" is correct. In this perspective, grammar is always relative, never absolute, and is likely to change with time and place. The descriptive grammarian is not judgmental about usage and draws no fixed conclusions about what people should do or should say and what they shouldn't do or say.

The one significant and overwhelming difference between these two schools of grammar is this: Prescriptive grammarians judge you by your grammar while descriptive grammarians do not. If you say "ain't" instead of "aren't," the prescriptive school of grammar will not only classify you as belonging to a certain class, it will also make assumptions about you and your background that are likely to be unflattering.

"So what?" you may ask. So plenty. You may not get that promotion you had hoped to get. You may find yourself shunted aside because the image your company wants to project does not mesh with your everyday misuse of grammar. Make no mistake about it: Grammar matters more than you think. What makes the influence of grammar even more damaging is that no one will ever tell you why you're really being held back. And if you ask, most people will try to put the best spin on things and blame something other than the real culprit—your bad grammar. Once that topic is opened, someone will have the uncomfortable job of explaining to you why your boss thinks it's out of place to answer the telephone by saying, "Mrs. Smith ain't here now, but she be back soon. Can I have her to call you?"

The tradition of judging people by their grammar is an ancient practice going back almost to the beginning of literacy. There's an old story about a wealthy merchant who, hoping to get his only son enrolled in a prestigious academy, took the boy to meet the philosopher who headed the school. The philosopher looked long and hard at the boy, who was standing not five feet away and clad in the finest clothes of the day, and said, "Speak, so I can see you." What did he mean? He meant that while clothes might help define (and sometimes disguise) the outer person, grammar expresses the real you—the soul—and once you open your mouth, there ain't no cover up possible.

A Peek at the History of English Grammar

Before the invention of English grammar books, a time of widespread linguistic chaos existed in which every writer pretty much wrote by personal rules of right and wrong created on the spot. Self-expression ruled the world; the common attitude among speakers and writers was "full speed ahead, damn the subject-verb agreement."

The first grammar book, as far as we know, was written in 1586 by one brave soul, an English printer by profession named William Bullokar. Misunderstanding among communicators was then at an epidemic. Although many of the English had by then learned how to read and write, the lack of an agreed-on grammar was threatening to overwhelm England with a universal babble.

Bullokar's contribution was *Booke at Large for the Amendment of English Orthographie (1580) with A Bref Grammar for English (1586)*. Reading it provided the reader with a 40-letter phonetic English alphabet. In 1762 a contentious man by the name of Joseph Priestley struck a decisive blow for English grammar by rejecting the centuries-old tradition of using the Latin model to explain English grammar. Priestley's answer was to collect into English the rules that most people were observing in their writing. His first brave little book was eventually followed by dozens and then hundreds of other English grammars, as teachers began to teach and use the same rules. As England expanded into the British Empire and became the focus of commerce all over the world, the demand for English grammars spread to foreigners who wanted to negotiate successfully in English, making them the first ESL students.

No single genius *invented* grammar; it simply developed from necessity. The rules of grammar today describe what and how the majority of educated people speak or write. No governor or king ever proclaimed that everyone must say, "You *were*" instead of "You *was*." But as long as educated people say, "You were" and not "You was," "were" will win out over "was."

Grammar continues to operate descriptively as well as prescriptively by providing English speakers and writers with the rules necessary for clear and consistent communication. Rules that were never intended to snobbishly earmark people into social classes now have that very side effect. Snobbery, however, was never the driving force behind the creation of a universal, standard English grammar. Our little grammar book assumes that you wish to speak and write with an educated slant because you want to be cool, not bullying. To that end, we'll try to make your journey as "cool" as possible.

2 THE ESL STUDENT AND THE NATIVE SPEAKER

DEFO! Y NOT CUM OVA 2MOZ. BTW OMG V SOZ 4 UR FRND. LMAO WOT A TTL SOB! :) ROFLMAO! G2G BEX LOL XX

www.CartoonStock.com

"But this is fantastic, professor! It's like no language I've ever seen before!"

Learning Objectives

- Explain what native and non-native speakers are

- Identify differences between native and non-native speakers

- Examine the three categories of difficulty for non-native speakers: pronunciation, homonyms, and idioms

Who speaks English as 2nd language?

Language typically consists of two main parts: sounds and rules. Its sounds are the way the language is spoken—its **pronunciation.** Its rules are its **grammar.** Of course, part of learning a language involves mastering the rules. But odd as it may seem, if you are a native English speaker, you already know, and correctly observe, many rules of the language simply because of the way it sounds. For example, do you see anything wrong with this sentence?

She will speaking with you later.

You probably noticed that the "be" is missing. The sentence should read, "She will be speaking with you later."

What about this sentence?

People in China is changing attitude toward having many childrens.

Certainly, you understand the intent of the comment, but most of you would word it this way:

People in China are changing their attitude toward having many children.

Because "People" is a plural noun, it requires the plural verb "are"; moreover, the plural form of *child* is *children,* not "childrens."

The fact is that if you are a native English speaker, you instinctively know more about your language than you think. For instance, did you know that practically every day, you use the future progressive tense? If you say you don't, you're wrong. The construction "She will be speaking" is in the future progressive tense. It is a very complex tense; yet you use it often and flawlessly, as you do many other tenses. Similarly, you do not need to know the formal definition of a preposition to correctly use one. Practically no native speaker would make this mistake:

Please place all books the table on.

It does not look right. But more important, it just does not sound right. The formal rule—that the preposition comes before the object it modifies— is one your ear prompts you to unconsciously practice. "Please place all books on the table" is what your ear would require.

Your ear for the language is so sensitive that it will immediately recognize any sentence or passage with words arranged in an unexpected order. For example, here is an actual letter from an overseas supplier to an American dentist:

Dear Doctor:

We happy enclosure of new kind of retainer, convincing that you and your office staff will like the new model. We also enclose a video with purpose to assist you in how to make the new retainer....

To your native ear, this snippet of writing will immediately sound odd because its phrasing is one no native speaker would use. Words are used in unfamiliar combinations, for example, "enclose a video with purpose to assist you." Here is one way someone with an ear for English might express the same idea:

Dear Doctor:

We are happy to enclose our new kind of retainer, convinced that you and your office staff will like the new model. We also enclose a video for the purpose of assisting you in making the new retainer....

One American student came back from an exchange trip to China and reported that he had seen the following sign posted in the baggage claim area of an airport:

Check you luggage. Don't mistake.

While the student grasped what the sign meant, he knew that in any English-speaking country, the proper wording would be the following:

Check your luggage. Don't mistake someone else's luggage for your own.

Your ear for the language, if English is your mother tongue, can be a useful tool in helping you become a fine writer.

Differences Between a Native Speaker and an ESL Student

Some basic differences exist between native speakers of English and ESL (English as a Second Language) students. Native speakers have heard the language spoken since infancy and have acquired an ear for it. ESL students have a similar ear for their own mother tongue, but not for English. Both can, however, learn to improve their English by using this book, even though their backgrounds with the language differ significantly.

Having an ear for a language means that you're usually able to tell when something doesn't sound right even if you can't say why. Nearly all native speakers have this ability. Most native speakers, for example, automatically say, "If I were you" without knowing the formal rule behind that expression. If an ESL student says, "If I were you," it is most likely because he or she has learned the formal rule of using the subjunctive.

ESL students, in short, face different challenges than do native speakers. The difficulties most ESL students have with learning English generally fall into three broad categories: **pronunciation, homonyms, and idioms.**

Pronunciation

Even the most meticulous speaker will occasionally flub the pronunciation of a word. How a speaker pronounces a word will vary with context, circumstances, and the speaker's accent. Some words in English take on a different meaning depending on how they are pronounced. To make matters worse, words often vary in meaning with the way they are pronounced. From experience, native speakers know, recognize, and use these differences almost instinctively. For example, place the emphasis on the first syllable of the word *present* and it means "a gift" as in, "Thank you for that awesome birthday present" or "a time period" as in, "There's no time like the present." However, place the emphasis on the second syllable of *present* and it means "to introduce" as in, "Ladies and gentlemen, I would like to present the President of the United States." Another example is the word *invalid.* If spoken with emphasis on the second syllable, the word means "legally flawed" as in the sentence "Her will was invalid." But when the emphasis is on the first syllable, *invalid* means "sick person" as in, "The invalid spent his days in bed."

Here are some other examples of meanings that depend purely on sound:

The lovely white <u>dove</u> flew from a branch just as I <u>dove</u> into the river.

Nancy was <u>close</u> to fainting, so the nurse asked that we <u>close</u> the door.

The <u>wind</u> was so powerful that the sailors could not <u>wind</u> the sails.

Many other examples of words whose meanings shift with pronunciation can be found in English.

PRACTICE 1

Working in a small group, explain the difference between the meanings of the underlined words in the following sentences.

1. His parents expected him to <u>progress</u> in college and to receive a good <u>progress</u> report.

   _____

2. He was too <u>deliberate</u> to <u>deliberate</u> thoughtlessly.

   _____

3. They <u>project</u> the <u>project</u> to cost nearly a million dollars.

   _____

4. The <u>bass</u> opera singer went fishing for <u>bass</u> in the lake.

   _____

5. The <u>entrance</u> to the garden was decorated so as to <u>entrance</u> visitors.

   _____

6. They want to <u>house</u> the visiting scouts in the headmaster's <u>house</u>.

   _____

7. With careful planning, they managed to <u>envelop</u> the plot in an <u>envelope</u> of secrecy.

   _____

8. He uses up all the <u>proceeds</u> from the banquet and then <u>proceeds</u> to pack his clothes.

   _____

9. They agreed to <u>reject</u> every <u>reject</u> from last year's applying class.

   _____

10. The delegates <u>bow</u> to the princess who wears a pink <u>bow</u> around her waist.

    _____

USAGE MONITOR

advise, advice

Both native and ESL students must learn to distinguish between these two words. *Advise* is a verb meaning "to suggest" whereas *advice* is a noun meaning "suggestion":

> You should *advise* her to walk home.

> If you follow your friend's *advice,* you'll lose money.

Here, pronunciation is the key to correctness: *Advise* is pronounced *ad-vīz* whereas *advice* is pronounced *ad-vīce.*

Homonyms

Homonym is the technical term for words that sound alike but differ in meaning. Here are some examples, with the homonyms underlined and explained in parentheses.

We <u>hear</u> that the entire country of Greece is going bankrupt. (are told)

Come over <u>here</u> so we can see your hat. (in this place)

The money burned a <u>hole</u> in his pocket. (a cavity or gap)

His cell phone caught the <u>whole</u> fight on camera. (complete, entire)

You could get a ticket if you don't <u>brake</u> for a disabled person crossing the street. (slow down)

A moose can <u>break</u> your leg with one mighty kick. (fracture, smash)

I fervently wish that Palestine and Israel would make <u>peace</u> with each other. (opposite of war)

Hey, buddy, I want a <u>piece</u> of that chocolate bar! (part, bit)

The meaning of a homonym is always determined by its spelling and context. Such odd words are more likely to confuse the ESL student than the native speaker.

USAGE MONITOR

Watch out for the Tricky Big Four sound alikes

Of all the mistakes made with homonyms by both ESL and native students, these four clusters stand out, so make sure you know the difference among all the words in each group.

Group 1: *it's, its*

<u>It's</u> my turn. (In this case, *it's* is a contraction for *it is*. *Note:* The only time you need an apostrophe is when you mean "it is.")

Hard work is <u>its</u> own reward. (You don't need an apostrophe because you don't mean "it is." *Its* is a pronoun showing possession.)

Group 2: *two, too, to*

Give me <u>two</u> pieces of bubble gum. (Not many of us mistake the number 2 for something else if we're concentrating.)

Jamison wants to visit Disneyland <u>too</u>. (Here, *too* means "also." *Note: Too* can also mean "excessive," as in, "Taking three exams per week was <u>too</u> much hassle.")

Bubba limped <u>to</u> the kitchen <u>to</u> see what kind of ice cream would be served. (The first *to* is a preposition meaning "toward"; the second *to* is part of the verb "to see.")

Watch how this cluster of three homonyms can be used in a single sentence: "Carry her <u>two</u> purses <u>to</u> the car unless it is <u>too</u> much trouble for you <u>to</u> walk that far." Did you understand the difference between the homonyms?

Group 3: *they're, their, there*

We know that three same sounds having three different meanings is frustrating, but the differences must be mastered for the sake of clarity.

Believe me, <u>they're</u> going to lose every last friend if they continue telling lies. (*They're* is always a contraction for "they are.")

Give me <u>their</u> cell phone number, just in case of an emergency. (*Their* is a possessive pronoun meaning "belonging to them.")

You will find the watch under that blue bag over <u>there.</u> (*There* means "in that place.")

<u>There</u> was never a better time to forward her e-mail. (*Note: There* is often used with forms of "to be," such as *there is, there are, there will be,* and so forth.)

Study the cluster of homonyms used in the following sentence and see if you understand the different meanings: "If no one shows up <u>there</u>, just leave the package on <u>their</u> doorstep and assume that <u>they're</u> on vacation—unless <u>there</u> is a sudden answer from inside the house."

Group 4: *you're, your*

These homonyms are frequently misused even by expert spellers. Actually, they are simple to keep straight if you just remember that *you're* is short for "you are" and that *your* means "belonging to you": *You're* irritating me with *your* sarcastic comments.

PRACTICE 2

Circle the correct homonym in parentheses. Use a dictionary if needed.

1. Her classroom behavior landed her in the (principle's, principal's) office.

2. When Ani got married, her father proudly walked her down the (isle, aisle).

3. Sometimes it feels good to (bear, bare) your soul.

4. The (assent, ascent) to the top of Mount Everest was deadly.

5. We need another long (board, bored) to make a picnic table.

6. Is it true that you (through, threw) a rotten tomato at your neighbor's dog?

7. That loud rock music is really testing my (patience, patients).

8. Don't let another selfish person (brake, break) your heart.

9. Why did they return all of those gorgeous wedding (presents, presence)?

10. We (new, knew) him as Billy the Bully.

Context and homonyms

A few homonyms are spelled and pronounced exactly the same, but you can determine their meanings on the basis of their **context.** Consider these examples:

> The burglar was shot by the police.
>
> After the sales meeting, my whole day was shot.
>
> He gave me a shot of whiskey.

From the context, most native speakers immediately grasp the different meanings of *shot* in these sentences. In the first example, *shot* means "gun-shot"; in the second, it means "ruined"; in the third, it means "measure" or "portion." Depending on how much or how little English they know, many ESL students would be puzzled by these shifting meanings.

Here are some other examples of words whose meanings change with context.

1. When he heard the news, he went into *shock.*
His freckled face was topped by a *shock* of red hair.

2. Let me just *lie* here on the green grass.
What that man just told you is a big *lie.*

In the first sentence, *shock* means a heavy blow of some kind; in the second, it means a thick mass. In its first use, *lie* means to be in a reclining position; in the second, it means an untruth.

PRACTICE 3

Working with a partner, define the underlined words, whose meanings change with context. Use a dictionary if you are stumped.

1. Be careful when you <u>cross</u> the road./She has her own <u>cross</u> to bear.

_____

2. They were married one month after they'd become <u>engaged</u>./The two countries <u>engaged</u> in war.

_____

3. He played the clarinet in a brass <u>ensemble</u>./She wore a stunning velvet <u>ensemble</u>.

_____

4. She was carrying a <u>parcel</u>./He told the girls to <u>parcel</u> out the treats.

_____

5. He threatened to <u>beat</u> her if she did not give him the money./I love the <u>beat</u> of her latest song.

_____

6. Their <u>spirits</u> were broken by constant harassment./She said she never drank any hard <u>spirits</u>.

_____

7. They looked for a home that would be <u>safe</u> from earthquakes./Keep your gold coins in a metal <u>safe</u>.

_____

8. The geology lecture was <u>hard</u> to understand./She said she adored <u>hard</u> candy.

_____

9. Her opinions are usually <u>objective</u>./Their <u>objective</u> is to complete the barn by winter.

_____

10. The landlord <u>left</u> in a huff./Turn <u>left</u> at the light.

_____

Grammar

English grammar can be troublesome. All of us occasionally come across constructions whose grammar seems suspect. Even professional grammarians often disagree about the rules of grammar, many of which sometimes appear downright ridiculous. The native speaker, who may not know formal grammar rules any better than the ESL student, at least has the advantage of being able to recognize the usual and customary places for nouns and verbs in a sentence. It is the rare native speaker, for example, who would say, "I to the store now go," putting the verb _go_ in the wrong place. Likewise, native speakers are unlikely to make prepositional errors such as saying, "Peggy stayed her room," leaving out the preposition _in_. The proper use of prepositions and articles is often a trouble spot for ESL students, however. An ESL student might say, "I must run to store," leaving out _the_, an error a native speaker is unlikely to make. ESL students whose first language is French or another romance language will typically refer to "the Smith or Brown," instead of "the Smiths or Browns." That is because in the French language, family names are never plural. Of course, native speakers do make grammatical errors; they're just more likely to make different kinds of errors than ESL students make.

The correct use of pronouns provides yet another headache for ESL students. A pronoun is a word used in place of a noun. ESL students may omit pronouns, as in the sentence "The students shouted when won the football game," which leaves out the pronoun _they_. Another tendency that ESL students have is to unnecessarily use both a noun and a pronoun to refer to the noun in the same sentence, as in, "My boss she increased my hourly pay." The ear of most native speakers would immediately detect this error.

Many foreign students, especially those from countries like China, Japan, and Russia, where the grammar of the native language is very different from English grammar, find it hard to write English correctly. We have had students complain in mournful tones, "I go over my writing again and again to make sure that I have corrected all grammar errors, but my teacher always finds more." Yet many millions of immigrants have arrived in America knowing absolutely no English and still mastered it well enough not only to survive, but to prosper.

This book teaches English grammar to both the ESL student and the native speaker. As we progress through the book, you will see our Usage Monitor! pop up whenever we feel that a native student's ear is an unreliable guide to a particular usage or when the ESL student needs to pay special attention. All rules will be accompanied by numerous drills.

This approach should help both types of students. The native speaker, who has the ear for English but perhaps not a grounding in its formal rules of grammar, will benefit from the extra practice. The ESL student, who may not have the native's ear but is learning the formal rules, will gradually become familiar with ordinary idiomatic usage. In either case, the goal is the same: for you to learn to write and speak English better. No matter which group you belong to, if you apply yourself to this book, you will gradually get better at both speaking and writing English.

PRACTICE 4

Using your ear or your grasp of the rules, correct the grammar of the following sentences. If the sentence is correctly written, mark a *C* beside it.

Example: Soon I must go bed. (Soon I must go <u>to</u> bed.)

1. When he was young, my father never go to school.

   _____

2. How can you believe such terrible lie?

   _____

3. Most Americans are proud of their many freedoms.

   _____

4. Last week I buyed a new car.

   _____

5. Mary should watch her wallet or it will be stealed.

   _____

6. Did you preregister at the Admissions Office?

   _____

7. By watching television, you can learn about many foreign country.

   _____

8. Which season of the year be your favorite?

   _____

9. The money in Laura's purse it added up to $100.00.

_____

10. When she shopping, she feels happy.

_____

Idioms

"fixing to"

An **idiom** is a phrase or expression that does not mean exactly what it says. The sentence "That guy is a fish out of water" means that he is in an uncomfortable position, not that he is a beached fish. Likewise, a woman who says, "It was raining cats and dogs" means that it was raining really hard, not that cats and dogs were falling from the sky. To say, "My best friend is in a pickle" means that your best friend is in some kind of trouble, not canned or bottled in preservatives or brine. Native speakers immediately get these meanings; ESL students may or may not, depending on their familiarity with such idioms.

To the ESL student, idioms can be a nightmare. The problem is that, while there is sometimes a natural logic to an idiom, just as often there is not. For example, to say that someone is a "fifth wheel"—meaning "unnecessary"—immediately brings to mind an image of uselessness, which is exactly what a fifth wheel would be, giving a natural logic to that particular expression. But what does "kick the bucket"—which means "to die"—have to do with dying? There was once a logical connection between the two. Kicking a bucket was a reference to suicide by hanging; a person would stand on a bucket to secure the noose, then kick the bucket out from under his or her feet. But this meaning has long been lost to most of us. What we are left with is an expression that is common in conversational English but means something totally different from what its individual words would suggest. That is the hallmark of an idiom.

It is not only the colorful phrases of idioms that ESL students find troublesome. What is also hard for them is learning how words are customarily grouped to make up conversational expressions. For example, we once heard a foreign student say to another who was about to take a test, "Have a good luck!" The student's meaning was clear, but a native speaker would have said, "Good luck!" In another example, an ESL student wrote in an essay, "I distorted my mind on this question," whereas a native speaker would write, "I changed my mind on this question." The phrase _distorted my mind_ is not technically wrong; however, it is not the customary idiomatic expression. Finally, a foreign speaker once said to one of the authors, "You're a neck in the pain!", another example of the type of error a native speaker is unlikely to make.

As another example of nonidiomatic English, here is an actual letter written by a European travel agent to an American client:

> I have received your dated fax May 3. I communicate to you that we are in accord on the appointment for Friday, May 25. We request you contact us the same day to be at the hour that is convenient. The place of the appointment, if you believe it opportune, can be in our office. Receive a cordial greeting as we transmit our best wishes.
>
> Manuel Ortega

No word in this brief letter is misspelled, and the grammar is not wrong. Still, the letter sounds foreign because the writer has not mastered idiomatic English. Rewritten in everyday English, the letter might sound like this:

> I received your fax dated May 3 and wish to confirm our appointment on Friday, May 25. We ask that you contact us on that day to arrange for a convenient meeting time. If you don't mind, we can meet in our office.
>
> Cordially, sending our best wishes,
>
> Manuel Ortega

As difficult as it might be, with practice and exposure to conversational English, both the ESL student and the native speaker will gradually gain mastery over the idioms of English.

PRACTICE 5

In the space provided, check the sentence that correctly uses idiomatic English.

1. ____ (a). Once in a blue moon, my sister writes me a letter.

   ____ (b). Once on the blue moon, my sister writes me a letter.

2. ____ (a). He blew up some steam by going to a movie.

   ____ (b). He blew off some steam by going to a movie.

3. ____ (a). I wish you would get the lead out and finish the job.

   ____ (b). I wish you would take the lead from your clothes and finish the job.

4. ____ (a). She looks like the spit of her mother.

   ____ (b). She is the spitting image of her mother.

5. ____ (a). He quit smoking cold turkey.

   ____ (b). He quit smoking like a cold turkey.

6. ____ (a). My sister is forever on the go.

   ____ (b). My sister on the go is forever.

7. ____ (a). For the love of Joseph, stop whining.

   ____ (b). For the love of Pete, stop whining.

8. ____ (a). No matter how educated you are, you should never talk down to other people.

   ____ (b). No matter how educated you are, you should never speak under other people.

9. ____ (a). Jim has never stopped living high on the hog.

   ____ (b). Jim has never stopped living on top of the hog.

10. ____ (a). I have awful hunger.

    ____ (b). I am awfully hungry.

PRACTICE 6

In the lines provided, write the meanings of the following idiomatic sentences.

1. He washed his hands of the problem.

_____

2. What a rat he turned out to be!

_____

3. That accusing look of his gives me goosebumps.

_____

4. When she was sixteen, her stomach was flat as a pancake.

_____

5. Frankly, my economics teacher bores me to death.

_____

6. Let's bury the hatchet and revive our friendship.

_____

7. He warned us that he would drop a bombshell at the meeting.

_____

8. I could tell by looking at her that the lights were on, but nobody was home.

_____

9. I searched my bedroom from stem to stern.

_____

10. She is as slow as molasses.

_____

11. At the crack of dawn, they packed up their sleeping bags.

_____

12. So, what's the bottom line?

_____

13. Don't count your chickens before they are hatched.

_____

Slang

Slang is informal speech or writing. It is almost never used in formal occasions and is frequently typecast as the language of the very young. But it is no exaggeration to say that every field or discipline has its own specialized slang that is used only by insiders or those in the know.

Most slang has the lifespan of a fruit fly. And many commentators believe that groups often exaggerate their slang to insulate their members from the rest of society. Your grandparents used *nifty, groovy,* or *right on* for good stuff, but *chill out, yucky,* or *jeepers creepers* for anything regarded as bad. Another chilling fact is that slang tends to die off with their users.

Yet some slang has had a surprising longevity, the best-known example being *OK*. This term began as part of a game played in the 1830s by newspapers in the Boston area. The idea was to come up with an abbreviation that did not fit and leave it to the readers to guess the correct meaning. *OK* was used as a humorous abbreviation for *all correct*—which it certainly wasn't. Fast-forward to the presidential election of 1840, with Martin Van Buren running for re-election. Taken from his birthplace of Kinderhook, New York, his nickname *Old Kinderhook* so perfectly matched the abbreviation that *OK* became one of his campaign slogans. *OK* survived; Van Buren, however, went down to a crushing defeat.

Some instructors regard slang as a source of pollution of the living language. We do not share this view. Conventional English is in no jeopardy of being drowned out by chatter from the street or corrupted by the babble of bookies. Language survives because it is at once both focused enough to describe the mutation of a virus and majestic enough for a prayer to the Almighty. Yet it has range enough to engulf and repel any assault on its traditions. Students today use *sick* to mean "marvelous, wonderful" and *cool* to mean "stylish" and "admirable." Let them call *Tophet* "balmy" if they wish (look up Tophet). Language will still be cool and will not bend or bow at these assaults. If language could answer these insolences, it would say in the words of a sports announcer at a roast given in his honor, "Gentlemen, you're throwing spit balls at a battleship."

 **Unit Test**

For each pair of sentences, check the sentence that is correct.

Example: _____ **(a).** Native speakers often have an ear for correct language but don't know the rules.

_____ **(b).** Nonnative speakers usually have a better ear for correct English than do native speakers.

1. Having an ear for the language means that

_____ **(a).** you're usually able to tell when something doesn't sound right.

_____ **(b).** you have a talent for learning new languages.

2. _____ **(a).** Language typically consists of sounds and rules.

_____ **(b).** Languages never differ in grammar.

3. _____ **(a).** The native speaker does not need to learn correct grammar.

_____ **(b).** The ESL student often has been trained in the formal rules of grammar.

4. _____ **(a).** Pronunciation is the way a word sounds.

_____ **(b).** Pronunciation is the way a word is spelled.

5. _____ **(a).** The word "wind" is always pronounced the same way in English.

_____ **(b).** The meaning of "wind" depends on how it is pronounced.

6. _____ **(a).** Homonyms sound alike but have different meanings.

_____ **(b).** Homonyms are words that originate from hymns.

7. _____ **(a).** The problem with slang is that it usually goes out of fashion.

_____ **(b).** Our grandparents never used slang.

8. _____ **(a).** The sentence "I love to look at moon" is grammatically correct.

_____ **(b).** The sentence "I love to look at moon" is grammatically incorrect.

9. _____ **(a).** The statement "I don't give a fig" is an exaggeration.

_____ **(b).** The statement "I don't give a fig" is an idiom.

10. _____ **(a).** When you cannot depend on your ear to figure out the correct English, you may benefit from extra drills.

_____ **(b).** When you cannot depend on your ear to figure out the correct English, assume that the rule is unimportant.

To check your progress in meeting this chapter's objectives, log in to **www.mywritinglab.com,** go to the **Study Plan** tab, click on **Sentence Basics** and choose **Standard and Non-Standard English** from the list of subtopics. Read and view the resources in the **Review Materials** section, and then complete the **Recall, Apply,** and **Write** sets in the **Activities** section.

3   THE BASIC SENTENCE

Learning Objective

- Identify elements of the basic sentence/parts of speech

www.CartoonStock.com

"MY INVENTION IS EVEN MORE REMARKABLE THAN YOURS. IT IS THE SIMPLE DECLARATIVE SENTENCE."

"When we read a sentence, we know who did what, or what happened and to whom."

A sentence is a group of words that expresses a complete thought. This completeness is what your speaker's ear uses to recognize a sentence. If someone said to you, "Match," you'd probably reply, "What?", meaning "What do you mean?" If, however, someone said, "I need a match to light the fire," you might reply, "Oh, let me find one." You'd respond differently because the second statement is complete enough for you to understand it. A sentence is made up of a group of words called the "parts of speech." We all remember elementary school when the teacher had us chant in unison, "A noun is the name of a person, place, or thing," "A verb shows action or state of being," "A pronoun takes the place of a noun," and so forth. The following chart summarizes all you need to know about the parts of speech. Review the chart until you understand how

21

each part functions. We shall have more to say about the parts of speech when we deal with the most common sentence errors (see Unit 7).

THE PARTS OF SPEECH AT A GLANCE

ENGLISH IS MADE UP OF EIGHT CLASSES OF WORDS CALLED "THE PARTS OF SPEECH": (1) *VERBS*, (2) *NOUNS*, (3) *PRONOUNS*, (4) *ADJECTIVES*, (5) *ADVERBS*, (6) *PREPOSITIONS*, (7) *CONJUNCTIONS*, AND (8) *INTERJECTIONS*. THE FOLLOWING CHART WILL CLARIFY THE FUNCTION OF EACH PART OF SPEECH:

NAME	FUNCTION	EXAMPLE
Verb	Shows action, occurrence, or state of being (inflections indicate tense and mood)	Jack *struck* the horse. The coat *fits*. Ann *is* happy. They demanded that she *move*.
Noun	Names a person, place, thing, idea, animal, quality, or action	*Lisa, Baghdad, chair, liberty, dog, friendliness, hesitation*
Pronoun	Takes the place of a noun and functions as a noun; pronouns can be personal, relative, indefinite, intensive, reflexive, demonstrative, or interrogative	Personal: *He* and *I* believe. Relative: A person *who* cares Indefinite: *Somebody* must pay. Intensive: *I myself* am fearful. Reflexive: They paid *themselves* big salaries. Demonstrative: *This* is better than *that*. Interrogative: *Who? What?*
Adjective	Modifies (restricts the meaning of) nouns or pronouns	A *pretty* girl, *Mexican* food, *its* color, *that* book, *the* word, *whose* pen, *larger* pieces
Adverb	Modifies (restricts the meaning of) verbs, adjectives, or other adverbs	He ran *quickly*. Max was *utterly* miserable. They played *unusually well*.
Preposition	Links a noun or noun substitute to another word in the sentence	An airplane flew *over, under, through, between, beyond, above* the clouds.
Conjunction	Connects words, phrases, clauses, and sentences	Coordinating conjunctions (*and, but, or, nor, for, so, yet*) connect items of equal rank: He hears, *but* he does not see. Subordinating conjunctions (*although, if, when, because, even though, since, until, when, while*) indicate a dependent clause and connect it with a main clause: *If* he calls, we shall answer.
Interjection	Expresses emotion	*Oh! Amazing! Ugh! Oops!*

PRACTICE 1

Attach the correct labels to the parts of speech in the sentences below.

Example: Dad gladly painted several chairs in the kitchen.

Dad: noun; *gladly*: adverb; *painted*: verb; *several*: adjective; *chairs*: noun; *in*: preposition; *the*: adjective; *kitchen*: noun.

1. "Ouch!" somebody hollered loudly and angrily in the room below us.
2. Betty is a woman who loves children and gives generously to them.
3. We insisted that Mike be honest because we knew his past record well.
4. That horrid hamburger and salad bothered my stomach considerably.
5. I wish you would stop leaving the door open behind you.

Notice that every word has a specific function in the sentence.

Subject and Verb

To be complete, every sentence must have a subject and a verb. In its simplest form, the **subject** is someone who does something:

> The <u>bird</u> sang.
>
> <u>Dick</u> shouted.
>
> <u>Mary</u> fell.

Naturally, the subject of a sentence can also be *something* rather than *someone*:

> The <u>car</u> stopped.
>
> The <u>bell</u> rang.
>
> <u>Jealousy</u> destroys.

The word that tells what the subject does or did is called the **verb.** From these examples, we know that the bird *sang*, Dick *shouted*, and Mary *fell*. We also know that the car *stopped*, the bell *rang*, and jealousy *destroys*.

Each of these examples is called a **kernel sentence.** A kernel sentence is the smallest sentence possible. Here are some other kernel sentences:

> Jump!
>
> Hurry!
>
> Watch out!

These kernel sentences are commands. The subject (you) is implied:

(You) jump!

(You) hurry!

(You) watch out!

Every sentence—no matter how long and complex—contains a kernel sentence. For example:

The bird sang.

Although we can add words to it, making it longer and more detailed, its kernel will still be *The bird sang.* Here are some examples with added words:

Early in the morning, <u>the bird sang</u>.

<u>The bird</u>, spreading its yellow wings, <u>sang</u>.

Despite black clouds and distant thunder, <u>the bird sang</u>.

<u>The bird sang</u> as if its heart were broken.

Perched on a tree limb, <u>the bird sang</u> until noon.

When we read a sentence, we know who did what or what happened and to whom. Therefore, to find the subject of a sentence, simply do this: First identify the verb. Then ask, "Who?" or "What?" in front of it. The answer will be the subject. So, for example, in the sentence *The bird sang,* we know that the verb is *sang.* If we ask, "Who sang?", the answer is the subject, *bird.*

PRACTICE 2

Underline the subject once and the verb twice in each of these sentences.

1. The man ate.

2. The clouds drifted.

3. The baby giggles.

4. The bomb exploded.

5. Knives cut.

6. The shoes pinched.

7. The heart stopped.

8. We waited.

9. Turkeys gobble.

10. The queen wept.

PRACTICE 3

Underline the kernel sentence in each of these sentences.

1. Greg leaped into the air.

2. Gathering yellow pansies, Marcia wandered away from the others.

3. The townspeople voted for the incumbent mayor.

4. The soccer players, victorious grins on their faces, left the field.

5. As the whole family sat down to dinner, she announced her divorce.

6. My hometown named our largest park after Ben Jones, who won a medal in the 1972 Olympics.

7. Jimmy cornered me in the drugstore.

8. Some hideous person stole three of our bikes.

9. Mr. Hightower ran down the road in his underwear.

10. Rain or shine, we walk at 6:00 every morning.

Every sentence contains a kernel sentence consisting of a subject and a verb.

Objects

Objects are words or groups of words governed by verbs or prepositions. You need to be able to distinguish between direct and indirect objects.

1. *The direct object* is any noun or pronoun that answers the question *What?* or *Whom?* after a verb. Here are some examples:

    Minda climbed the *wall*. (She climbed *what*?)

    Mom embarrassed the *postman*. (She embarrassed *whom*?)

Notice that a direct object can also follow gerunds, participles, and infinitives (see the "Verbals" section on pp. 33–36 for more about these grammatical forms).

> *Buying* (gerund) a *house* (object) takes money.
>
> That boy *smoking* (participle) a *cigarette* (object) is my cousin.
>
> *To grow* (infinitive) *melons* (object) is his goal.

USAGE MONITOR

Prepositions always require the objective case of pronouns

> For *him*, between you and *me*, behind *them*, under *us*.

Many Americans habitually use the wrong pronoun. Don't allow your ear to trick you into making common errors such as these: "Between you and I, the United States is too tolerant," "The phone rang for her and I," or "If you have questions, speak to Karen or myself."

Here are the correct versions: "Between you and me, the United States is too tolerant," "The phone rang for her and me," "If you have questions, speak to Karen or me."

2. *The indirect object* states *to whom* or *for whom* (or *to what* or *for what*) something is done. In other words, an indirect object names a person or thing that is indirectly acted upon. Usually an indirect object is followed by a direct object. Here are some examples:

The manager gave *her* (indirect object) the wrong *letter* (direct object).

I always leave *waiters* (indirect object) a big *tip* (direct object).

PRACTICE 4

Underline the direct object in each sentence that follows.

1. He handed John a flag.
2. Using her cell phone was the fastest way.
3. The company gave pay raises to all of the workers.
4. Let's contact the student leaders.
5. To dream bad dreams is possible.
6. Behind me stood another gentleman.
7. The old man refused to live without her.
8. The generals studied every map intensely.
9. Chewing tobacco, he muttered, "Howdy."
10. Marco willingly gave the villagers his help.

PRACTICE 5

Underline the indirect object in each sentence that follows. If the sentence has no indirect object, move on to the next sentence.

1. My parents left me beautiful memories.
2. He contracted the measles from his little brother.
3. The quarterback threw Murphy the ball.
4. We have no food to give him.
5. The hot weather scorched the land from north to south.
6. He rode his bicycle while she drove her car.
7. She brought him the wrong coat.
8. Realizing one's potential gives one self-esteem.
9. May God grant our country peace and prosperity.
10. Yes, we bought our tickets yesterday.

Prepositional Phrases *Time or space*

Sometimes it's easy to spot the subject of a sentence, but other times it isn't. For example, what is the subject of this sentence?

One of Mary's friends gave her a surprise party.

If we apply the test of asking, "Who?" before *gave,* we find that *One* is the subject. Because the prepositional phrase *of Mary's friends* comes before the verb *gave,* you might mistake *Mary's friends* for the subject.

A **preposition** is a word that shows the relationship between two things; a prepositional phrase is a group of words beginning with a preposition. A preposition always has an **object**—usually a noun or pronoun that follows it. The preposition and its object make up the prepositional phrase. Here is an example:

Ginger placed the napkin <u>in the napkin ring</u>.

Here the preposition is *in,* and the object is *napkin ring.* Remember this formula:

PREPOSITION	+	OBJECT	=	PREPOSITIONAL PHRASE
on		the table		on the table
to		the sea		to the sea
of		the college		of the college
from		the store		from the store

Below is a list of the most common prepositions:

about	beside	inside	to
above	besides	into	toward
across	between	like	through
after	beyond	near	throughout
against	by	of	under
along	despite	off	underneath
among	down	on	until
around	during	out	up
at	except	outside	upon
before	for	over	with
behind	from	past	within
below	in	since	without
beneath			

USAGE MONITOR

One trick that will help you remember how prepositions work is to think of all an airplane can do when approaching a cloud. It can fly *beside, inside, above, into, toward, across, through, underneath, around, outside, over, behind, past, within, below,* or *beneath* the cloud. A few prepositions, such as "about," "despite," or "except," won't fit this scheme, but you get the idea.

One way to avoid mistaking a preposition for the subject of a sentence is to cross out the prepositional phrases in any sentence whose subject you're trying to find. Here are some examples:

> The captain of the team encouraged the players.

> The subject is *captain,* not *team.*

> The top of the mountain could not be seen.

> The subject is *top,* not *mountain.*

Notice: A prepositional phrase consists of a preposition and its object.

PRACTICE 6

Cross out the prepositional phrase(s) in each of the sentences below. Then identify the subject by circling it.

1. Tom went up the block and down the street.
2. After the lecture, we went into the Orange Room for coffee.
3. She ran out the door without her keys.
4. I'll have a chocolate sundae with fudge sauce and nuts on top.
5. She backed into the driveway without wearing her glasses.
6. We turned into the left lane and stopped at the next light.
7. From the other side we watched.
8. Fred walked around the tent and into the woods.
9. We waited in the lobby for Nick and Steffie, but they were already in their seats.
10. During the night, snow drifted against the door.

PRACTICE 7

Create a prepositional phrase for each of the following prepositions. Then use it in a complete written sentence.

1. on

_____

_____

_____

2. under

_____

_____

_____

3. without

_____

_____

_____

4. from

_____

_____

_____

5. near

_____

_____

_____

6. between

_____

_____

_____

7. behind

_____

_____

_____

8. off

_____

_____

_____

9. like

_____

_____

_____

10. throughout

_____

_____

_____

Action Verbs and Linking Verbs

Verbs tell us who did what action in a sentence. However, what about a verb like *is*? What action does *is* describe? In fact, it describes no action because *is* is a linking verb.

There are two main kinds of verbs: action verbs and linking verbs. **Action verbs** describe an action. They tell us that the subject did a particular something. Here are examples:

> Jack answered the question.
>
> The dog chewed the bone.
>
> Jerry served the drinks.

A **linking verb** connects the subject to other words that say something about the subject. Here are some examples:

> My family is poor.
>
> Grandpa looks happy.
>
> The cheese smells bad.
>
> That music sounds odd.

The linking verb *is* connects the subject *family* to the word *poor*, which is the family's condition. Likewise, *Grandpa* is linked to *happy* by the linking verb *looks*, *cheese* to the word *bad* by the linking verb *smells*, and *music* to the word *odd* by the linking verb *sounds*. Linking verbs are said to be *linking* because they *link* the subject to words that tell us something about the subject.

SOME COMMON LINKING VERBS

am	sound
are	look
has been	appear
is	seem
was	taste
were	smell
feel	

Some linking verbs can also act as action verbs, depending on their role in the sentence. Here are some examples:

To smell

Linking:	That cheese *smelled* rotten.
Action:	The rat *smelled* the cheese.

To taste

Linking:	The strawberries *taste* sweet.
Action:	The soldiers *taste* the water.

PRACTICE 8

Circle the linking verb(s) in each of the following sentences.

1. Addictions are dangerous.
2. Missy is a tiny parakeet.
3. Harry Pendergast was my dad's banker.
4. Her car looked old and battered.
5. Most people appear honest.
6. The apple pie tastes as good as it looks.
7. College freshmen often feel insecure.
8. The sky looks overcast.
9. Cheeseburgers are popular everywhere.
10. My cousin has always been my best friend.

USAGE MONITOR

good, well

Good is an adjective and therefore describes only nouns ("It's a *good* rug"). *Well* is an adverb and describes verbs, adjectives, and other adverbs (e.g., "She sings *well*"). *Well* is used as an adjective only when it means *good health.* If someone asks you, "How are you?", don't answer, "I'm *good,* thank you." Answer, "I'm *well,* thank you. The rule is simple: *Good* is always an adjective, but it does not apply to one's health. *Well* is always an adverb, but it is used as an adjective when it describes good health.

Helping Verbs

Verbs sometimes need additional words to express the past, present, and future. These additional words are called **helping verbs.** In the sentences that follow, the **complete verb** is underlined.

The teachers <u>are meeting</u> at noon.	**(Present)**
The teachers <u>will meet</u> at noon.	**(Future)**
The teachers <u>had met</u> before noon.	**(Past)**
The teachers <u>were meeting</u> when the fire alarm rang.	**(Past)**
The teachers <u>have been meeting</u> all week.	**(Past)**
By tomorrow, the teachers <u>will have met</u>.	**(Future)**

Here, for example, are some of the many forms of the verb *eat.* Notice the many different helping verbs.

eats	should have been eating	would have eaten
ate	can eat	should have eaten
is eating	would have been eating	must have eaten
was eating	will be eating	having eaten
may eat	had been eating	did eat
should eat	have eaten	had eaten
will eat	has eaten	does eat
will have eaten		

When we form questions, we often use the helping verbs *did, do,* or *does,* as in the following examples:

<u>Did</u> you finish your work? ("Did finish" is the verb.)

<u>Do</u> bears eat worms? ("Do eat" is the verb.)

<u>Does</u> the peach taste sour? ("Does taste" is the verb.)

Occasionally, words that are not part of the complete verb will come between the helping verb and the main verb. Here are some examples:

She has <u>definitely</u> registered.

Many students had <u>already</u> taken the course.

A flashlight would <u>certainly</u> help.

In summary:

- There are two main kinds of verbs: action verbs and linking verbs.

- Helping verbs are additional words that help express the tense of a verb.

PRACTICE 9

Underline the complete verb in the following sentences.

1. She will be going to Perimeter College next year.

2. The seamstress should have charged more.

3. Marie is sweeping the porch right now.

4. Did they remember his generosity?

5. As always, Mother was cooking enough for an army.

6. The renters should have signed their lease.

7. The horses were galloping toward the barn.

8. They could have waited for Heather.

9. He may be in his room.

10. They must have decided to get rid of the photos.

PRACTICE 10

In the following sentences, underline the helping verb once and the main verb twice. Underline only the complete verb(s). Do not underline words that come between the helping verb and the main verb.

1. We must always tell the truth.

2. She has often driven Aunt Betty to the doctor.

3. The stock market should have quickly rallied.

4. Women should have voted centuries ago.

5. The smart person will never repeat idle gossip.

6. They had really hoped she would leave the next day.

7. The groundhog could have quickly disappeared down the hole.

8. Jessica had easily answered all the questions on the test.

9. The new coach has just arrived.

10. The souvenir shop will not return your money.

Verbals

Verbals are words that look like verbs, but do not act like verbs. Verbals are of three kinds: gerunds, participles, and infinitives. We'll look at each separately.

Gerunds

Gerunds are words that end in *-ing* and act as nouns. How can you tell if an *-ing* word is a gerund or a verb? Easy: Look for the helping verb. For an *-ing* word to be a verb, it must have a helping verb. Look at these sentences:

We were studying.   **(*were* + *-ing* = verb)**
Studying is hard.   **(*Study* + *ing* + subject = gerund)**

Apply the test for a subject by asking, "Who?" or "What?" before the verb. What *is hard*? *Studying*. In other words, *studying* = subject = gerund.

PRACTICE 11

Write *V* when the *-ing* word is used as a verb, and circle the helping verb. Write *G* when the *-ing* word is used as a gerund.

1. We have been driving around the city.

2. Both girls were licking an ice cream cone.

3. Lending money to friends can cause disappointment.

4. Jack is organizing his backpack.

5. Getting all *A*'s would be terrific.

6. He is losing his battle against obesity.

7. Walking is good exercise.

8. Driving a car is a necessity in the United States.

9. He has been bothering his girlfriend.

10. Avoiding work is no solution.

Participles

Participles are words that look like verbs but act like adjectives, meaning that they describe. Present participles end in *-ing*. Past participles end in *-ed*. Here are some examples:

Ginny is marrying Jack.	(*is marrying* is a verb identifying what Ginny is doing)
Jack is a marrying man.	(*marrying* is a present participle describing the man Jack)
We chopped the onions.	(*chopped* is a verb telling what we did to the onions)
The chopped onions will add flavor.	(*chopped* is a past participle describing the onions)

PRACTICE 12

In the following sentences, identify participles with a *P* and verbs with a *V.*

Example: *P* Most barking dogs are not angry.

       V Fritz is barking for food.

1. ____ The banging shutter woke us up.

    ____ Fred is banging on the door.

2. ____ The creek is still running by our house.

    ____ Running water damaged our roof.

3. ____ The sandwich tastes like soaked cardboard.

    ____ We soaked the dirty clothes in bleach.

4. ____ Why are detergents always "new and improved"?

    ____ Johnny improved his test scores.

5. ____ Several bored teenagers hung around the music store.

    ____ That film bored me to death.

6. ____ By playing with the thread, she tangled it.

    ____ Liz had difficulty combing her tangled hair.

7. ____ Frightened, he climbed into bed.

    ____ The earthquake frightened our entire neighborhood.

8. ____ Tell everyone to get out of the blistering heat.

    ____ The radiation was blistering his skin.

9. ___ They had been marching all day.

___ Have you received your marching orders yet?

10. ___ The right front fender had been dented.

___ Let's throw away that dented teapot.

Infinitives

Infinitives consist of *to* plus a verb. Infinitives *never* act as verbs but always serve some other function. Study these examples:

Suzy preferred to suffer alone.	**to suffer tells what Suzy preferred; the verb is preferred**
He wanted a place to study.	**to study tells what kind of place; the verb is wanted**
She vowed to get their respect.	**to get tells what she vowed; the verb is vowed**

Be careful not to confuse an infinitive with the preposition *to* followed by a noun or a pronoun.

Infinitive:	Jennifer decided to skip the party.
Preposition:	Jennifer went to the party.

USAGE MONITOR

Prepositions again

Here's a useful shortcut to memorizing verbals:

Verbals—words that look like verbs but do not act like verbs—come in three kinds: gerunds, participles, and infinitives.

- Gerunds act as nouns.
- Participles act as adjectives.
- Infinitives consist of *to* plus a verb.

PRACTICE 13

Underline only the infinitives in the following sentences. Do not underline if *to* is a preposition.

1. How do you expect to win?

2. I plan to offer the job to Jim.

3. Don't forget to visit your elderly aunt.

4. We prefer to walk to the library.

5. Many students try to cram for tests.

6. He hesitates to drive at night.

7. I ran to see what had happened to her.

8. They did not want to risk their reputations for him.

9. Just cut some string and bring it to me.

10. Peter's pulse began to quicken.

PRACTICE 14

Underline the verb and circle the infinitive in the following sentences.

Example: The wind <u>began</u> to blow.

1. We are expecting to settle in Kentucky.

2. All the mothers preferred to stay with their children.

3. Her brother likes to tease her.

4. All of us would like to speak fluent English.

5. Try to keep all the tickets in one envelope.

6. He will certainly have to apologize.

7. To be happy is not my main goal in life.

8. He insisted on his right to leave the country.

9. I plan to cook dinner on Monday.

10. Bullets, real and psychological, aim to kill.

Compound Subjects and Verbs

A sentence with more than one subject is said to have a **compound subject.** Here are some examples:

> Mary and Madeline shopped.
>
> The woman and her dog ran.
>
> My roommate and I argued.

A sentence may also have more than one verb—called a **compound verb.** Here are some examples:

> Mary walked and shopped.
>
> The woman waved and yelled.
>
> My roommate huffed and puffed.

Compound subjects and verbs may appear in the same sentence:

> Mary, Helen, and Isa walked and shopped.
>
> The woman and her friend waved and yelled.
>
> My roommate and I argued, made up, and laughed.

PRACTICE 15

Underline the compound subjects in the following sentences.

1. My boss and his daughter came to my birthday party.

2. Politeness and civility seem to be characteristics of the past.

3. Spaghetti, a green salad, and fresh bread are my favorite meal.

4. A fool and his money are soon parted.

5. Museums, monuments, and castles invite tourists to visit them.

6. Bears, wolves, foxes, and other wild animals should be protected.

7. Newspapers and magazines are great to read on the airplane.

8. Looks plus talent are a good combination.

9. Love and marriage go together like a horse and carriage.

10. Action and freedom are an important part of U.S. history.

PRACTICE 16

Underline the compound verbs in the following sentences.

1. The crook staggered and disappeared.

2. Expensive gifts often surprise and embarrass their recipients.

3. The French king captured the throne and governed the people.

4. She arched her brows and smiled.

5. We stood in line and talked.

6. Shawna made breakfast and walked the dog.

7. Michael jumped from the car and ran into the house.

8. The vine climbed and curled along the fence.

9. She delicately peeled and ate the orange.

10. Ronnie slept and snored all night.

 **Unit Test**

In the following paragraph, underline all subjects once and all verbs (including helping verbs) twice. Circle the verbals (gerunds, participles, and infinitives).

I love to visit Lucinda's Bonjour Café. Everyone should have a private oasis of that kind—a warm, comforting place. Bonjour Café is not an elegant restaurant like restaurants uptown with thick carpets, damask drapes, and someone to check your overcoat. It is just a cozy, clean little shop with a display cabinet full of fresh pastries and a coffee machine for making great cappuccinos. The motley clientele includes all kinds of old people from the retirement home across the street, small business owners renting in the neighboring mall, and people simply wanting to break up their day with a fresh, homemade lunch. Lucinda owns and operates the shop. She is the reason it attracts such a faithful clientele. Lucinda's warm hospitality and her French effervescence are a strong magnet. She goes out of her way to be kind to those frail oldsters limping in on walkers, and she never forgets to ask people about the good or bad events in their lives. My closest friends and I love to meet at Bonjour for lunch or for an afternoon snack. Lucinda will be there to welcome us like long-lost members of her family.

To check your progress in meeting this chapter's objectives, log in to **www.mywritinglab.com,** go to the **Study Plan** tab, click on **Sentence Basics** and choose **Parts of Speech and Subjects and Verbs** from the list of subtopics. Read and view the resources in the **Review Materials** section, and then complete the **Recall, Apply,** and **Write** sets in the **Activities** section.

4 BUILDING SENTENCES

www.CartoonStock.com

*"Some say I shouldn't be so picky,
which is why I'm not going to stop
seeing you for ending a sentence
with a preposition."*

Learning Objectives

- Write and identify sentence parts and complete sentences

- Define and write the three basic sentence types (simple/compound/complex) along with statements, questions, commands, and explanations

- Understand sentence variety

*"Writers seldom write with only one sentence type
for the same reason that good cooks season their
food with more than just salt."*

Every sentence must have a subject and a verb. To this rule there is no exception. Not every construction with a subject and verb, however, is a sentence. It could instead be a **dependent clause.**

Dependent and Independent Clauses

A **clause** is a group of words with both a subject and a verb. If a clause makes sense on its own and is a complete sentence, it is called an **independent clause.** The following are independent clauses and, therefore, complete sentences:

> He cleaned his glasses.
>
> They took the bus home.
>
> We are saving money for a vacation.

What about the following examples?

> When he cleaned his glasses
>
> If you take the bus
>
> While we saved money for a vacation

Each of the above clauses has a subject (*he, you, we*) and a verb (*cleaned, take, saved*), but none makes complete sense. Each is a **dependent clause**—a group of words with a subject and verb that must be connected to an independent clause to make sense.

> John could see the crack when he cleaned his glasses.
>
> If you take the bus, get off at Maple Street.
>
> While we saved money for a vacation, we didn't feel deprived.

Your ear for language is the best judge of whether a clause makes sense and whether it is independent or dependent. Many dependent clauses begin with a telltale sign—one of these words:

who	which
whom	that
whose	

These words are called **relative pronouns.** They have that name because they show how a dependent clause is *related* to a main clause.

A dependent clause may also begin with one of the following words, called **subordinating conjunctions:**

after	if	so that	whenever
although	in order that	than	where
as if	now that	that	wherever
because	once	though	whether
before	provided that	unless	while
even if	rather than	until	why
even though	since	when	

USAGE MONITOR

affect, effect

These two words confuse more students than you can imagine, so let's make sure you know the difference between them. *Affect* means "influence or change": "Panicky citizens can *affect* the stock market." *Effect* is the result of something: "Her giggle had a pleasant *effect* on the audience." In brief, something *affects* you; therefore, it has an *effect* on you.

Typically, it is a subordinate conjunction that makes a clause dependent. In fact, removing the subordinate conjunction changes a dependent clause into an independent one. Here are some examples:

Dependent:	Until you forgave him.
Independent:	You forgave him.
Dependent:	Because you served on the jury.
Independent:	You served on the jury.

ESL Advice!

If you don't trust your ear to be able to distinguish a dependent from an independent clause, look for the presence of a relative pronoun or subordinate conjunction. Either one will help you identify the construction as a dependent clause.

PRACTICE 1

In the blanks provided, write *D* if the clause is dependent and *I* if the clause is independent. For each clause you label *D*, underline the word that makes the clause dependent.

1. —— Who spoke with a high, nasal voice.

2. —— He imagined himself walking down the street.

3. —— The cover was torn and dirty.

4. —— Although no one spoke.

5. —— Rather than covering up the mistake.

6. —— They stood there with their hats on.

7. —— Because it is such a beautiful day.

8. —— That she decided to become a nun.

9. —— If war could have solved the problem.

10. —— The temptation is to rush.

PRACTICE 2

In each blank, write an independent clause to complete the sentence.

1. _____, who won first prize.

2. If you agree, _____.

3. _____, where I collapsed from fatigue.

4. Now that he has graduated, _____.

5. _____ while watering the lawn.

6. Before you give him the gift, _____.

7. While I'm trying to finish the story, _____.

8. _____whenever he opens his mouth.

9. If we ask him to join us for lunch, _____.

10. _____where we finally found a piece of land for sale.

Three Basic Sentence Types

There are three basic sentence types: simple, compound, and complex. All three sentence types are commonly used in writing and talking. We will discuss each separately.

The simple sentence

A **simple sentence** consists of a single independent clause. First graders routinely write simple sentences such as these:

> I like Billy.
>
> Peggy is mean.
>
> Butch bit me.

But the simple sentence, in spite of its name, is not always short, crisp, and childlike. It can be expanded if given more than one subject or verb. Here are some examples:

Simple sentence with more than one subject:	The hens and chicks scratched for bugs.
Simple sentence with one subject and three verbs:	Too many people speak without thinking, read without understanding, and work without goals.

Another way to expand the simple sentence is to add **modifiers,** words that describe or explain the subject or verb. Here are some examples:

Simple sentence:	The chicken scratched for bugs.
First expansion:	The chicken, a big, beautiful Rhode Island Red, scratched for bugs.
Second expansion:	The chicken, a big, beautiful Rhode Island Red, scratched for bugs in the dusty barnyard.

PRACTICE 3

Expand the simple sentences below by adding subjects, verbs, or modifiers.

1. The bed is old.

   _____

2. The wife took the stand.

   _____

3. The old man sat on the bench.

   _____

4. A book can be a good friend.

   _____

5. My cousin throws money away.

   _____

6. Foolish friends are a burden.

   _____

7. To face reality is sometimes difficult.

   _____

8. The two cars crashed.

   _____

9. My aunt tells wonderful stories.

   _____

10. All the foods I like are fattening.

   _____

The compound sentence

A **compound sentence** consists of two or more simple sentences joined by a coordinating conjunction. There are seven **coordinating conjunctions:** *and, but, for, or, nor, so,* and *yet.* The simple sentences in a compound sentence should express ideas of equal importance. Here are some examples:

Simple:	Comic strips entertain. Sermons inspire.
Compound:	Comic strips entertain, and sermons inspire.
Simple:	Jason must get some sleep. He will get sick.
Compound:	Jason must get some sleep, or he will get sick.
Simple:	He was athletic. He didn't practice. He lost the match.
Compound:	He was athletic, but he didn't practice, so he lost the match.
Simple:	She had never ridden a bicycle. I had not either.
Compound:	She had never ridden a bicycle, nor had I. (Notice the change in subject and verb order in a *nor* clause.)

Notice that a comma comes immediately before the coordinating conjunction that joins the sentences.

PRACTICE 4

Use a coordinating conjunction to join each pair of simple sentences into a compound sentence. Write your answers below the simple sentences.

Example: Money is important. Money can create greed.

Money is important, but it can create greed.

1. The dog fetched the bone. Those watching enjoyed the sight.

_____

_____

2. I telephoned my grandmother. I congratulated her on her 75th birthday.

_____

_____

3. I have dieted for one month. I have not lost any weight.

_____

_____

4. The doctor made a house call. He had forgotten his medical bag.

_____

_____

5. John will straighten up the living room. It will look good for company.

_____

_____

6. Give me a big hug. I need to feel loved.

_____

_____

7. The moon is bright and golden. We should go for a walk.

_____

_____

8. I have studied all day. I still don't feel ready for the test.

_____

_____

9. Everyone has left. The room is empty.

_____

_____

10. I drank some strong coffee. Now I can't sleep.

_____

_____

The complex sentence

The **complex sentence** consists of one or more independent clauses joined to one or more dependent clauses. Unlike the compound sentence, which connects two equal ideas, the complex sentence emphasizes one idea over the other. The less important idea is said to be *subordinate*. Naturally, the more important idea is expressed in the independent clause:

> Alicia's heart is broken because her sweetheart left.

Alicia's broken heart is the main idea; the less important idea is why it is broken (because her sweetheart left).

Common sense and your ear for language will help you decide which of two ideas is more important and which therefore belongs in the independent clause. Here are, for example, two sentences:

> I hung out the American flag. I went to the post office.

If you want to emphasize *going to the post office,* you will put it in the independent clause:

> After I hung out the American flag, I went to the post office.

If you want to emphasize *hanging the American flag,* you will put it in the independent clause:

> Before I went to the post office, I hung out the American flag.

Bear in mind the words that signal a dependent clause. You may wish to review the relative pronouns and subordinating conjunctions on pages 57–58 before you do the exercises.

PRACTICE 5

Join the following sentences into complex sentences using a relative pronoun or subordinating conjunction. Be sure to express the more important idea in the independent clause.

Example: Anger causes suffering. Indifference is even worse.
Although anger causes suffering, indifference is even worse.

1. I congratulated Henry. He was pleased.

_____

2. We are at a crossroads. We shall succeed or fail.

_____

3. I bought a Chevrolet. It has more room than a Honda.

_____

4. We need a curfew on our street. The noise pollution is terrible.

_____

5. She acts very mature. She is the youngest.

_____

6. He put down the heavy box. He rang the doorbell.

_____

7. Skydiving is exciting. It is extremely dangerous.

_____

8. Children often feel responsible for their parents' divorce. They suffer guilt.

_____

9. Moving away can be difficult. It often means losing old friends.

_____

10. I love suspense movies. They keep me awake at night.

_____

PRACTICE 6

Write a series of sentences on one of your favorite activities—something you really enjoy. Each sentence should be of the specific type listed below.

1. Simple sentence with more than one subject:

_____

2. Simple sentence with more than one verb:

_____

p.43   **3.** Simple sentence with modifiers:

_____

4. Two compound sentences:

  (a). _____

  (b). _____

5. Three complex sentences:

  (a). _____

  (b). _____

  (c). _____

PRACTICE 7

Exchange papers with a classmate and discuss the sentences you wrote in Practice 6. Help each other make any necessary corrections.

USAGE MONITOR

among, between

Are we being picky? No, we're just being pernickety. Use *among* when you're referring to three or more things: "The rumor was circulated *among* all 50 math majors."

Use *between* when discussing two things: "The final race was *between* von Bonhote and Lopez."

Statements, Questions, Commands, and Exclamations

So far, we've been discussing sentences as grammatical units and classifying them according to their structure. But sentences can also be classified by purpose. Sentences, whether simple, compound, or complex, do not always make straightforward statements. Sometimes they ask questions, give commands, or offer exclamations. Here are some examples:

Simple statement:	The table has not been set.
Simple question:	Has the table been set?
Simple command:	Set the table immediately!
Simple exclamation:	How nicely the table is set!
Compound statement:	Charities receive a lot of money, and they have an obligation to use it wisely.
Compound question:	Do charities receive a lot of money, and do they use it wisely?
Compound command:	Sir, your charity has received a lot of money, but stop wasting it!
Compound exclamation:	How amazing to realize the huge amount of money charities receive and how often they waste it!
Complex statement:	Because diabetes causes heart disease, it is life threatening.
Complex question:	If diabetes causes heart disease, is it life threatening?
Complex command:	Let's cure diabetes because it is a life-threatening disease.
Complex exclamation:	How sad it is to realize that 20 million people are at risk of becoming seriously ill each year because diabetes is a life-threatening disease!

PRACTICE 8

In the space provided, label the following sentences with *S* for simple, *C* for compound, and *X* for complex.

Example: *X* Was she crying because he left?

1. _____ Get out and never come back!
2. _____ If the dog bites you, will you sue the owner?
3. _____ Why is Ariana so determined?
4. _____ How beautifully the lake shimmers and how mysteriously it laps the shore!
5. _____ Although you are tired, will you help me?
6. _____ Why does Bill sleep so much and how does he make a living?
7. _____ Drop that stick, you monster!
8. _____ The sun is shining, so will you go for a walk with me?
9. _____ Raise your hand if you dare!
10. _____ How bitter he has become!

Sentence Variety

Writers seldom write using only one sentence type for the same reason that good cooks season their food with more than just salt. Any sentence pattern that is overused will quickly seem boring. Variety is the key to a good writing style and can be achieved easily if you use a mix of simple, compound, and complex sentences. The following is a ho-hum passage:

> Rap music started during the 1970s. It comes from African chanting. It also comes from chatting. Rap music means "chat music." It contains rhythmic statements.

The passage consists of a string of simple sentences. Notice how it is immediately improved when the sentence types are varied:

> Rap music, which started during the 1970s, comes from African chanting. It also comes from chatting. Rap music means "chat music," and it contains rhythmic statements.

Here is another passage that suffers from lack of variety:

> I looked at my desk. I groaned at the pile of incomplete assignments on it. They had stacked up for a week. I had kept delaying my studies.

Here is the same thought improved by variety:

> I looked at my desk and groaned when I saw the pile of incomplete assignments on it. They had stacked up for a week because I had kept delaying my studies.

This sort of sentence variation is exactly what you instinctively do in your everyday talking. It is what you must also try to do in your writing.

PRACTICE 9

Rewrite the following paragraph to eliminate the choppy effect of too many simple sentences. Read the sentences aloud to determine the relationship between them. Then reduce the number of simple sentences by combining some into compound and complex sentences.

> Hairdressers often function as therapists for their clients. They listen to all kinds of personal confessions. I have my hair cut once a month. I am always surprised by what I overhear. Once I heard a woman literally broadcast her husband's affair. She told the entire salon. She was speaking above the noise of the blow-dryer. She was not aware of how loud she was. I have pondered why such intimacy exists between hairdressers and clients. For one thing, hairdressers are service oriented. They are kind to their clients. Also, hairdressers do not belong to most clients' normal social groups. Hairdressers can be objective. They can be uninvolved listeners. Many hairdressers understand human nature. They offer good advice. They offer practical advice. They can help with personal problems.

Unit Test

1. Write a simple sentence with modifiers about the clothing you are wearing today.

2. Write a complex sentence beginning with *Although.* Be sure to place a comma following the dependent clause.

3. In the spaces provided, identify whether the sentence is simple (*S*), compound (*C*), or complex (*X*).

   _____ **(a).** Before we arrive home, let's count the money.

   _____ **(b).** Think hard, and you will find the answer.

   _____ **(c).** This pottery, which is made by Hopi Indians, is expensive.

   _____ **(d).** When I receive your letter, I'll answer it.

   _____ **(e).** This is a dull, gray morning, but the sun is peeking through the clouds.

4. In the paragraph that follows, underline all **dependent** clauses.

   Parents must preach what they practice. They must not preach morality that they themselves ignore. For instance, Peggy's parents constantly tell her to be more frugal and to quit buying clothes that sit unused in her closet. I find that rather ironic since Peggy's mother wears a different outfit every day and buys only from Neiman Marcus, Saks Fifth Avenue, or some other expensive store. How can Peggy absorb the message of frugality from a spendthrift mother? Then there are my friend Ray's parents. Because they want him to become a lawyer, they criticize him whenever he gets a *C*. They don't let him go out more than once on a weekend. "You won't get into law school," they say. But I never see Ray's parents without a glass of beer or Scotch in their hands. They drink all the time. Now, what kind of hypocrisy do we have here? We have parents who preach a gospel of hard work and deprivation while they party. One basic principle of child rearing is this: Parents must preach only those moral principles that they themselves observe.

5. Rewrite the following paragraph to eliminate the choppy effect of too many simple sentences.

Train watching is an old tradition. It is an American tradition. We do not use trains the way people do in Europe. In Europe people regularly use trains for transportation. They travel from city to city by hopping on a train. But here in the United States, trains are relatively rare. Perhaps that is why people love to watch trains. Retired men especially love to watch trains. They love to watch trains arrive. They love to watch trains depart. My hometown is Glendale, California. My hometown has a strong tradition of train watching. Every morning a group of men gathers at the Metrolink Station. They gather soon after dawn. These men have little in common. What they do have in common is their love for trains. To them, watching trains is wonderful entertainment. Watching trains is cheap, too. They watch freight trains. They watch passenger trains. Every train has its special attraction. When it rains, these men sit in their cars. They watch from the driver's seat. That isn't as much fun. They would rather stand at the rail. They would rather talk about the trains. They would rather talk about the train's exotic destinations. The men have a nice camaraderie. There is another perk to being a train watcher. The train engineer gives an extra toot on the whistle as a train passes. He acknowledges this special band of spectators.

To check your progress in meeting this chapter's objectives, log in to **www.mywritinglab.com,** go to the **Study Plan** tab, click on **Sentence Basics** and choose **Sentence Structure and Varying Sentence Structure** from the list of subtopics. Read and view the resources in the **Review Materials** section, and then complete the **Recall, Apply,** and **Write** sets in the **Activities** section.

PART TWO

THE 20 MOST COMMON SENTENCE ERRORS

What is an error in English grammar usage? You would think that this is a rhetorical question—meaning, one that is asked but never intended to be answered. In fact, it is a reasonable question, given the state of English grammar in the world today. Probably few beliefs are more polarizing than certain usage idols in English that are widely used as benchmarks of social class. Use these benchmark elements of "good English," and many flattering assumptions will be made about you, your background, and the social class to which you supposedly belong. Yet often there is no good or logical reason for preferring one expression over another.

Take, for example, the split infinitive, which is a construction that inserts a word between "to" and the verb. Many people think that this usage is absolutely wrong. Probably the most commonly used example of a split infinitive in popular culture is the stated mission of the *Star Trek* starship *Enterprise,* namely "*to boldly go* where no man has gone before." Purists insist that the correct version is "boldly to go" or "to go boldly."

The founder of the rule concerning **split infinitives** was an 18th-century amateur grammarian and clergyman by the name of Robert Lowth, whose 1762 publication *A Short Introduction to English Grammar* laid down some silly principles of English usage that persist to this day. Lowth is responsible for "different from" being considered chic and correct while "different to" or "different than" is regarded as bad English. Some of his rulings were arbitrary; others were just preposterous. In the case of the split infinitive, Lowth, foremost a Latin grammarian, reasoned that since the infinitive in Latin is always a single word—such as *pugnare,* "to fight,"—its English equivalent must also never be split.

If this were an argument on French usage, it would eventually have been taken up by the Academie Francaise, founded in 1635 by Cardinal Richelieu as the purity police of French. However, no such certifying authority exists in the English language, leaving individual experts, dictionaries, and institutions to slug out the differences. This is essentially what happened, with this addition: While the French were busy sealing their intellectual borders against the poison gas of English expressions like *du weekend,* English, with its rough-and-tumble, open admission to all **forms of expression,** stealthily replaced French as the primary worldwide language of diplomacy and aviation.

From the students' point of view, the lack of a certifying authority in English has made learning the language somewhat chaotic. But it could be worse. You could end up like the French grammarian on his deathbed, whose last words were, "I am about to—or I am going to—die; either expression is **proper usage.**"

1 SENTENCE FRAGMENTS

THE FIRST SENTENCE FRAGMENT

www.CartoonStock.com

Learning Objectives

- Identify different types of sentence fragments and how they are caused

- Learn how to correct each type of sentence fragment

A **sentence fragment** is only part of a sentence. It is a "wannabe" sentence that lacks either a subject, a verb, or sense. Sometimes the omission occurs because the writer is "on a roll" and flying across the page. It's fine to write fast and get all your thoughts down in a hurry, but then you must always proofread for errors.

Here are some examples of fragments:

Lost his wallet.	**(Missing subject)**
Mary's job.	**(Missing verb)**
Despite his charm.	**(Missing sense)**

A fragment can spring from one of several causes. If you learn to recognize them, you will be able to avoid fragments in your own writing.

Fragments Due to a Missing Subject

When you include the verb but forget to write the subject, the result is a fragment. Here are some examples:

Lenny made a date with Fern. Then never showed up.

After the party they had double milk shakes. Also apple pie.

In these examples, the writer mistakenly thought that the subject of the first sentence also applies to the second group of words. It does—but the second thought must be formally joined to the first by a conjunction such as *and* or *but*. If you forget the conjunction, you must write the two thoughts as separate, complete sentences.

Lenny made a date with Fern, but he never showed up.

or

Lenny made a date with Fern. However, he never showed up.

After the party they had double milk shakes and apple pie.

or

After the party they had double milk shakes. They also had apple pie.

PRACTICE 1

Correct the following fragments resulting from a missing subject. You can either join the fragment to the preceding sentence or rewrite the fragment as a separate sentence.

1. The children were excited. And ran into the gym.

_____

_____

2. Murphy found out that he was adopted. Then searched for his biological mother.

_____

_____

3. Grandma put on the rented ice skates. Stood up and let go of the railing. And started to skate as if she were still a teenager.

_____

_____

4. He locked the door. Or at least thought he did.

_____

_____

5. The courtship was passionate. But burned out in two months.

_____

_____

Fragments Due to a Missing Verb

Each complete sentence must have a verb. Most fragments are unintentionally created when part of the verb is left out. Verbs such as *is* or *are* and helping verbs can be omitted in certain foreign languages, but they must appear in English. "Frogs not princes" is a fragment, not a full sentence, whereas "Frogs *are* not princes" is a full sentence. "You received a ticket this year?" is missing its helping verb; therefore, it is a fragment. "*Have* you received a ticket this year?" is a full sentence.

PRACTICE 2

In the blank provided below, place the letter of the line from the second column that will correct the fragment.

1. —— spending money foolishly these days.

2. —— sure that you like me.

3. —— always chasing after pretty girls.

4. —— called *Lepidoptera* by professional gardeners.

5. —— as romantic as fall?

(a). Butterflies are

(b). Too many people are

(c). I have never been

(d). Lud is

(e). Is winter

Answers:
b, c, d, a, e

Fragments Due to *-ing* Words

Some fragments are triggered by an *-ing* word such as *puffing* or *playing*. Here are some examples:

> He sat there with contentment. Puffing on his cigar.

> I remained at my desk. Playing with some yellow Silly Putty.

Why beginning with an *-ing* word often leads to a fragment is something of a puzzle. Possibly, the writer mistakes the *-ing* word for a full verb, which it isn't.

To correct a fragment due to an *-ing* word, either join it to the preceding sentence (use a comma to set off the first part of the sentence), or rewrite it as a separate sentence:

> He sat there with contentment, puffing on his cigar.

> I remained at my desk, playing with some yellow Silly Putty.

> > or

> He sat there with contentment. He puffed on his cigar.

> I remained at my desk. I played with some yellow Silly Putty.

PRACTICE 3

Correct the *-ing* fragments by rewriting the sentences below.

1. The lions slept in the sun. Snoring contentedly.

_____

_____

2. Max and I stood at the bus stop. Waiting for Joe.

_____

_____

3. Dad loves soy sauce. Pouring it on everything.

_____

_____

4. Judy loves to create romance. Using candlelight for every dinner she cooks.

_____

_____

5. I am a registered Democrat. Voting often, however, for Republican legislation.

_____

_____

Fragments Due to *To* Phrases

A fourth common type of fragment is triggered by *to* phrases. Two examples follow:

> We are in the process of saving money. To pay our bills.

> Melany bought a newspaper. To see if the Trojans had won the game.

As before, you can correct this type of fragment by either joining it to the preceding sentence or rewriting it as a separate and complete sentence:

> We are trying to save money to pay our bills.

--------------------- or ---------------------

> We are trying to save money. We want to pay our bills.

> Melany read the newspaper to see if the Trojans had won the game.

or

> Melany read the newspaper. She wanted to see if the Trojans had won the game.

Note that you could also move the *to* clause to the beginning of the combined sentence. If you do this, put a comma after the *to* clause.

> To pay our bills, we are trying to save money.

> To see if the Trojans had won the game, Melany read the newspaper.

PRACTICE 4

Correct the following *to* fragments by either joining them to the preceding sentences or rewriting them as separate sentences.

1. The students went on a trail hike. To clean up the environment.

_____

_____

2. Hogs are trained to root around on the forest floor. Looking for truffles.

_____

_____

3. He wanted desperately to persuade her. To quit calling him "Snooky."

_____

_____

4. She stood outside the office trying to summon up enough nerve. To speak to her professor.

_____

_____

5. Try to get some spirit and loyalty. To cheer the team on.

_____

_____

Fragments Due to Dependent Words

You have learned about fragments caused by omitted subjects, omitted verbs, *-ing* words, and *to* clauses. You have also learned two main ways of correcting fragments—by joining the fragment to the preceding sentence or by rewriting the fragment as a separate sentence.

Now we will learn about a fifth kind of fragment, one that is triggered by misused relative pronouns and subordinate conjunctions. There is only one way to correct this fifth type of fragment: by joining it to the preceding sentence. Here is a list of relative pronouns that can create fragments:

who　　　　whose　　　　that

whom　　　which

Here are examples of fragments created by unconnected relative pronouns:

> We looked at the flat tire. <u>Which</u> was beyond repair.

> We have a week to pay our landlord, Mrs. Smith. <u>Who</u> has been most patient.

Here are the corrections:

> We looked at the flat tire, which was beyond repair.

> We have a week to pay our landlord, Mrs. Smith, who has been most patient.

As you can see, both fragments were corrected by joining them to the preceding sentence. Indeed, both resulted from the writer's use of a period instead of a comma.

A fragment can also be triggered by the misuse of a subordinate conjunction. As with relative pronouns, this type of fragment can be corrected in only one way—by joining it to the preceding sentence. Here is a list of subordinate conjunctions:

after	although	as if
because	before	even if
even though	if	in order that
now that	once	provided that
rather than	since	so that
than	that	though
unless	until	when
whenever	where	wherever
whether	while	why

Here are some examples of fragments resulting from unconnected subordinate conjunctions:

> <u>Although</u> his desk is messy. He runs a well-organized program.

> <u>Wherever</u> he lives and works. Discord breaks out.

To correct such fragments, simply join them to the neighboring sentence:

> Although his desk is messy, he runs a well-organized program.

> Wherever he lives and works, discord breaks out.

Note that if the dependent clause comes first, it is separated from the independent clause by a comma:

Incorrect: Because it was raining. We brought along our umbrellas.

Correct: Because it was raining, we brought along our umbrellas.

Or: We brought along our umbrellas because it was raining.

PRACTICE 5

Rewrite each of the following fragments by joining it to the neighboring sentence.

1. Even though the old roof is leaking. We are not getting a new one.

   _____

   _____

2. She bought a new watchband. That looks very expensive.

   _____

   _____

3. Ask him about his family. If you see pictures of children on his desk.

   _____

   _____

4. Find out more about his background. Before you hire him.

   _____

   _____

5. Purchase one good outfit each season. Rather than a dozen cheap ones.

   _____

   _____

Fragments Due to Added Details

Details added to a sentence can also create a fragment. Beware of the words listed below. They often lead to added-detail fragments.

especially	including
except	not even
particularly	such as
in addition	for example

Here are three examples of fragments created by added details:

No one knew exactly what they were feeling. Not even the boss.

They won several prizes. Including a trip to Hawaii, a new car, and a refrigerator.

Abraham Lincoln saw violence as the supreme threat to America. Particularly war.

To correct a fragment resulting from added details, simply attach the details to the previous sentence, adding any words necessary. Use a comma to set off the added details.

No one knew exactly what they were feeling, not even the boss.

They won several prizes, including a trip to Hawaii, a new car, and a refrigerator.

Abraham Lincoln saw violence as the supreme threat to America, particularly war.

If the additional-detail fragment is long, you can make it into a separate sentence:

Fragment: Fred tends to antagonize people because he acts like a real jerk. For example, never being on time, talking only about himself, interrupting others, and talking with his mouth full.

Corrected: Fred tends to antagonize people because he acts like a real jerk. For example, he's never on time, and he talks only about himself, interrupts others, and talks with his mouth full.

PRACTICE 6

Correct the following added-detail fragments by joining them to the preceding sentence.

1. Rick is so paranoid he's put three locks on his door. In addition to installing a security system.

_____

_____

2. She can't stand to be touched. Except by her own sister.

_____

_____

3. I suffer from allergies all year round. Ragweed, tree mold, and dust.

_____

_____

4. We gave her some excellent suggestions for staying out of debt. Including creating a budget.

_____

_____

5. A major problem of our industrialized world is job boredom. Such as the boredom of factory assembly jobs.

_____

_____

Error 1 Review

The following paragraph contains fragments. Correct each error using one of the methods you have learned.

I often wonder how old people manage to stay happy. Especially when their health fails. One afternoon I expressed this wonderment to my 85-year-old grandmother. Because I felt it important to find an answer. She was in her wheelchair. Having suffered a broken hip last year. I sat in a chair next to her. Thinking about how frail she had gotten. Though I didn't really know exactly what words to use. I finally took courage and asked, "Grandma, how do you handle being confined to a wheelchair? When you were always so active?" She thought for an instant. Then she said, "Getting old is not for sissies. Not even for people who are not sissies. Especially if you have lost your health and mobility. But, as long as I have my mind, I can enjoy something every day. For instance, your visit right now. It's such fun to hear about your college life. Particularly the classes you are taking and the friends you are making." What she was really telling me was that people have to make the best of their situation. Which is true at any age. Not just when you're old. I felt inspired by her attitude.

USAGE MONITOR

Remember that a complete sentence always has a *subject* and a *predicate*. Don't be floored by the Latin word *predicate*. It just means "predicts"—or tells—what the subject is doing or experiencing.

To check your progress in meeting this chapter's objectives, log in to **www.mywritinglab.com,** go to the **Study Plan** tab, click on **The 20 Most Common Sentence Errors** and choose **Fragments and Combining Sentences** from the list of subtopics. Read and view the resources in the **Review Materials** section, and then complete the **Recall, Apply,** and **Write** sets in the **Activities** section.

ERROR

2 RUN-ON SENTENCES

A **run-on sentence** is actually two sentences written as one. There are two main types of run-on sentences: the fused sentence and the comma splice.

The **fused sentence** consists of two sentences joined—or *fused*—without any punctuation between them:

> We drove to Las Vegas it is an exciting city.

Here is how the sentence should be written:

> We drove to Las Vegas. It is an exciting city.

USAGE MONITOR

If you read a run-on sentence out loud, you should notice a necessary pause that requires end punctuation.

The second type of run-on sentence is the **comma splice**—two full sentences separated by a comma instead of a period:

> We took a day trip to Hoover Dam, it's so impressive.

Here is the sentence, corrected:

> We took a day trip to Hoover Dam. It's so impressive.

Learning Objective

- Understand the two types of run-on sentences and the different methods for correcting them.

PRACTICE 1

In the blanks provided, write *FS* if the run-on sentence is a fused sentence and *CS* if it is a comma splice. Then correct the error in the lines following the sentence.

1. _____ Stop talking to me I have no time for this.

_____

_____

2. _____ You must be on time, he will be angry if you aren't.

_____

_____

3. _____ Golf is a very hard game it is probably the hardest game of all.

_____

_____

4. _____ It was a lovely evening, there wasn't a cloud in the sky.

_____

_____

5. _____ Take the bus save gas money.

_____

_____

6. _____ Stand firm and be patient then get busy with your life.

_____

_____

7. _____ It slithers and twists, it must be a snake.

_____

_____

8. _____ He entered the house, immediately he began to smell the cheese odor.

_____

_____

9. _____ The United States is a large country we still have more land than people.

_____

_____

10. _____ I would like to live to be one hundred, I would be spanning a century.

_____

_____

Correcting Run-On Sentences

There are four ways to correct run-on sentences. Take, for example, this sentence:

I'm in a good mood you are in a better mood.

To correct it, you can do one of the following:

- Put a period at the end of the first sentence.

  I'm in a good mood. You are in a better mood.

- Put a semicolon at the end of the first sentence.

  I'm in a good mood; you are in a better mood.

- Put a coordinating conjunction at the end of the first sentence (note that a comma goes before the conjunction).

  I'm in a good mood, but you are in a better mood.

- Use a subordinating conjunction (note that a comma is placed between the two clauses).

  Though I'm in a good mood, you are in a better mood.

Note that no comma is needed if the independent clause comes first, as in the example that follows:

  I'm in a good mood though you are in a better mood.

PRACTICE 2

Correct the following run-ons in all four possible ways.

1. He missed his plane he had to take a later flight.

   Insert a period: _____

   Insert a semicolon: _____

   Insert a coordinating conjunction and comma: _____

   _____

   Insert a subordinating conjunction and comma: _____

   _____

2. I like to play chess I'm no good at the game.

   Insert a period: _____

   Insert a semicolon: _____

   Insert a coordinating conjunction and comma: _____

   _____

   Insert a subordinating conjunction and comma: _____

   _____

3. I'll go to the bookstore we can take your car.

   Insert a period: _____

   Insert a semicolon: _____

> **Insert a coordinating conjunction and comma:** _____
>
> _____
>
> **Insert a subordinating conjunction and comma:** _____
>
> _____

4. She lived for a while in Mexico she was not happy there.

Insert a period: _____

Insert a semicolon: _____

Insert a coordinating conjunction and comma: _____

_____

Insert a subordinating conjunction and comma: _____

_____

5. Many men have courted Cathy none has been successful.

Insert a period: _____

Insert a semicolon: _____

Insert a coordinating conjunction and comma: _____

_____

Insert a subordinating conjunction and comma: _____

_____

PRACTICE 3

Correct the following run-on sentences using one of the four possible ways.

1. Jennifer is a lucky person she should play the lottery.

_____

_____

2. The political season is upon us, there are daily ads on television for the candidates.

_____

_____

3. Worms are beneficial to the soil they are everywhere.

_____

_____

4. Shoplifting is not just a nuisance crime it is paid for by honest shoppers.

_____

_____

5. Speeding is a common traffic offense it is not as bad as reckless driving, though.

_____

_____

6. My landlord is very punctual he's always on time to collect the rent.

_____

_____

7. Don't sneeze on me, I don't want your cold.

_____

_____

8. I'm madly in love with my neighbor she doesn't even know I exist.

_____

_____

9. Men are vainer than women they just hide it better.

_____

_____

10. Many people read for pleasure, on the other hand, more people read for business.

_____

_____

Error 2 Review

The following paragraph contains fused sentences and comma splices. Correct each error in any way you choose.

One summer I worked as a lifeguard at the local pool, I found the job surprisingly difficult. Chief among my difficulties was keeping the roughhousing kids in line, especially the teenagers, I found that frequently they would defy my authority. Since I was a teenager myself, it was a constant struggle to control them, I had to really put my foot down. One day an incident occurred that taught all of us a lesson. Some boys were horsing around in the deep end, dunking each other and splashing I told them to stop but they wouldn't listen they kept right on, churning up the water and disturbing other swimmers I yelled at them repeatedly. Finally, I said to myself, that's it, this has to stop and it has to stop right now. I got off my lifeguard stand and went down to the pool deck to really let them have it when I thought I saw the vague outline of a submerged swimmer. I screamed at the boys to stop their splashing they screamed right back at me. I dove in they started to splash me, too, but in spite of all the foam I swam to the bottom, found an unconscious swimmer, and brought him to the surface. While someone called the paramedics, I worked on the boy the other teenagers suddenly become very serious they stopped all the horsing around. By the time the paramedics arrived, I had pumped most of the water out of the victim's lungs he was conscious and talking. He said he had had a seizure because of all the splashing he had been unable to attract attention and get help. For the rest of the summer, those boys never gave me any more trouble I think they realized that they had almost caused someone to drown.

To check your progress in meeting this chapter's objectives, log in to **www.mywritinglab.com,** go to the **Study Plan** tab, click on **The 20 Most Common Sentence Errors** and choose **Run-Ons and Combining Sentences** from the list of subtopics. Read and view the resources in the **Review Materials** section, and then complete the **Recall, Apply,** and **Write** sets in the **Activities** section.

ARE YOU THE NEW ENGLISH TEACHER?

YES I ARE!

EDGAR ARGO

www.CartoonStock.com

Learning Objectives

- Explain and understand singular and plural subject-verb agreement

- Review common subject-agreement errors

Subjects and verbs must agree in number: That is the one rule of subject–verb agreement. A singular subject always takes a singular verb; a plural subject always takes a plural verb. Most of the time, this rule is clear and easy to follow, as in the following sentences:

Peggy admires Fred.

The workers admire Fred.

Peggy, a singular subject, takes the singular verb *admires. Workers,* a plural subject, takes the plural verb *admire.*

We are also likely to come across sentences like these:

He don't want company.

There is pickles in the refrigerator.

69

He, a singular subject, is incorrectly paired with the plural verb *don't.* *Pickles,* a plural subject, is incorrectly paired with the singular verb *is.*

Subject–verb agreement errors are typically caused by some common words and grammatical situations. Here they are, in no particular order:

- *Do, don't, was,* and *wasn't:*

  Incorrect: He don't remember his promise.
  Correct: He doesn't remember his promise.

  Incorrect: You was right again.
  Correct: You were right again.

- *Each, every, either/or,* and *neither/nor:*

  Incorrect: Each of us are to blame for the mistake.
  Correct: Each of us is to blame for the mistake.

  Incorrect: Either of the shirts are the right size.
  Correct: Either of the shirts is the right size.

- Prepositional phrase between a subject and verb:

  Incorrect: One of the three television sets are broken.
  Correct: One of the three television sets is broken.

- Sentences beginning with *there/here:*

  Incorrect: There is too many potatoes to peel.
  Correct: There are too many potatoes to peel.

  Incorrect: Here is the best solutions to the problem.
  Correct: Here are the best solutions to the problem.

- Questions:

  Incorrect: Where is the warm blankets?
  Correct: Where are the warm blankets?

- Compound subjects joined by *and, or, either/or,* or *neither/nor:*

  Incorrect: The doctor and nurse was talking.
  Correct: The doctor and nurse were talking.

  Incorrect: The doctor or the nurse were upset.
  Correct: The doctor or the nurse was upset.

- The indefinite pronouns *each, everyone, anybody, somebody,* and *nobody:*

  Incorrect: Each of the passengers wish to get off here.
  Correct: Each of the passengers wishes to get off here.

- *Who, which,* and *that:*

  Incorrect: Larry is one of those people who gives cheap gifts.
  Correct: Larry is one of those people who give cheap gifts.

We'll take up these situations one by one.

USAGE MONITOR

kind, sort

Kind and *sort* are singular and should always be used with *this* or *that:*

> *This kind* of meat tends to be expensive. *That sort* of paint has an oil base.

Kinds and *sorts* are plural and should be used with *these* or *those:*

> Let's avoid *those kinds* of movies. *These sorts* of roses have orange petals.

Do, Don't, Was, and *Wasn't*

Subject–verb disagreements are often caused by the words *do, don't, was,* and *wasn't.* Here are the correct forms of *to do:*

SINGULAR	PLURAL
I do	We do
You do	You do
He, she, it does	They do

Here are examples of agreement errors made with *do* and *don't:*

Incorrect: She do her assignments on time.

Correct: She does her assignments on time.

Incorrect: He don't realize what time it is.

Correct: He doesn't realize what time it is.

Was and *wasn't* are also involved in many subject–verb agreement errors. Here are the correct forms:

SINGULAR	PLURAL
I was	We were
You were	You were
He, she, it was	They were

Here are some examples of errors commonly made with this verb:

Incorrect: You was in the kitchen.

Correct: You were in the kitchen.

Incorrect: They was eating taffy apples.

Correct: They were eating taffy apples.

PRACTICE 1

Underline the correct verb in parentheses in the following sentences.

1. They (was, were) sitting in the bleachers.

2. That answer (doesn't, don't) make sense.

3. (Wasn't, Weren't) you already up by 6:30 this morning?

4. Donna, you (was, were) supposed to get dessert.

5. Matthew (doesn't, don't) always act on principle.

Each, Every, Either/Or, and *Neither/Nor*

The words *each, every, either,* and *neither* all take a singular verb. Here are some examples:

> Each dog, cat, and owner <u>was</u> (not *were*) listed by name.
>
> Every skirt and blouse <u>is</u> (not *are*) being ironed and folded.
>
> Neither of the senators <u>votes</u> (not *vote*) for more college funds.
>
> Either of the photos <u>is</u> (not *are*) flattering to her.

Don't be confused by the prepositional phrase—for example, *of the photos*—that usually follows *each, every, either,* or *neither.* Cross it out and the verb choice will be clear.

Either/or and *neither/nor* are also trouble spots. Here are some examples:

> **Incorrect:**   Either the teacher or the student were in the wrong.
> **Correct:**   Either the teacher or the student was in the wrong.
>
> **Incorrect:**   Neither the pitcher nor the catcher were any good this season.
> **Correct:**   Neither the pitcher nor the catcher was any good this season.

If one subject joined by *either/or* or *neither/nor* is singular and one is plural, the verb should agree with the nearer subject.

> **Incorrect:**   Either the coyotes or our dog bark all night.
> **Correct:**   Either the coyotes or our dog barks all night.
>
> **Incorrect:**   Either our dog or the coyotes barks all night.
> **Correct:**   Either our dog or the coyotes bark all night.

PRACTICE 2

Underline the correct verb in parentheses in the following sentences.

1. Neither of the sandwiches (has, have) mayonnaise.

2. Each of the contestants (hold, holds) a little flag.

3. Every house on the block (is, are) blue.

4. Either the criminal or the victims (is, are) being interviewed now.

5. Neither the cherries nor the apricots (has been, have been) picked.

Prepositional Phrases Between a Subject and Its Verb

A prepositional phrase that comes between a subject and verb can result in an agreement error. Here is a list of common prepositions:

about	along	behind	between
above	among	below	beyond
across	around	beneath	by
after	at	beside	despite
against	before	besides	down
during	near	past	underneath
except	of	since	until
for	off	through	up
from	on	throughout	upon
in	out	to	with
inside	outside	toward	within
into	over	under	without
like			

Here is a typical agreement error created by a prepositional phrase coming between a subject and a verb:

> Only one of his many movies have won an Oscar.

The prepositional phrase *of his many movies* comes between the subject *one* and the verb *have*. However, the subject is still *one,* and *one* is always singular. Cross out the prepositional phrase, and the subject is immediately clear:

> Only one has won an Oscar.

PRACTICE 3

Cross out all prepositional phrases in the sentences that follow. Then circle the subject and underline the correct verb.

1. The bicycles leaning against the ladder (is, are) for sale.
2. The sheets on the bed (look, looks) like silk.
3. That box of cans and bottles (go, goes) to the recycling center.
4. Out of season, a pound of cherries (costs, cost) more than $5.
5. The vase on the piano (is, are) filled with pink silk flowers.

Sentences Beginning with *There/Here*

Subject–verb agreement errors can easily occur in sentences that begin with *there is, there are, here is,* or *here are.* Here are some examples:

Incorrect:	There <u>was</u> three women sitting in the back row.
Correct:	There <u>were</u> three women sitting in the back row.
Incorrect:	Here <u>is</u> the black buttons to sew on my coat.
Correct:	Here <u>are</u> the black buttons to sew on my coat.

In all these examples, the writer is confused by *there* or *here,* which strike the ear as singular. Neither *here* nor *there,* however, is the subject of the sentence. If you're confused by such sentences, reword them to make the subject come before the verb, and the mistake will quickly become visible.

> Three women were sitting in the back row.

> The black buttons to sew on my coat are here.

PRACTICE 4

Underline the correct verb in parentheses. Circle the subject.

1. Here (is, are) Linda Palmer's application.
2. There (is, are) the Colorado Rockies.
3. There (is, are) times in life that try my soul.
4. Here (is, are) the books you requested.
5. There (was, were) two clouds on either side of the rainbow.

British English — group

Questions

Most sentences that we write or speak are statements, such as these:

> The stars are out.

> The apple is green.

In these, and in most statements, because the subject comes before the verb, it is easy to spot an agreement error.

On the other hand, when we ask a question, the verb typically comes before the subject:

> Where are the stars?

> What color is the apple?

With the subject following the verb in a question, it is easy to make an agreement error, such as this one:

> When is Keith and Samantha leaving?

In order to use the correct plural verb *are,* a speaker or writer must guess that a plural subject—*Keith and Samantha*—lies ahead. Sometimes we guess wrong.

If you're in doubt about the subject–verb agreement in a question, simply reword it as a statement. So, for example, we have:

> Keith and Samantha (is/are) leaving soon.

It is now evident that the plural *are* is the correct verb since *Keith and Samantha* refers to two people.

PRACTICE 5

Underline the correct verb form in the following questions.

1. Who (is, are) those men standing on the corner?

2. When (do, does) Simone and Mary arrive?

3. Where (is, are) the knives and forks?

4. How many raffle tickets (has, have) Marvin sold?

5. Why (was, were) the fans cheering?

Compound Subjects Joined by *And, Or, Either/Or,* or *Neither/Nor*

Sentences that include this construction can give writers trouble:

singular noun + and + singular noun

Here are some examples:

The bride and groom looks happy.

Luck and hard work is a winning combination.

Cobwebs and dirt covers the window.

In each of these sentences, the writer was fooled by what seems to be a singular subject. However, just as one plus one make two, one singular subject plus another singular subject joined by *and* always make a subject plural. The sentences should therefore read:

The bride and groom <u>look</u> happy.

Luck and hard work <u>are</u> a winning combination.

Cobwebs and dirt <u>cover</u> the window.

Although two singular subjects joined by *and* always take a plural verb, two singular subjects joined by *or* require a singular verb:

Steak and chicken <u>are</u> on the menu.

but

Steak or chicken <u>is</u> on the menu.

Burt and Gus <u>are</u> driving to Florida.

but

Burt or Gus <u>is</u> driving to Florida.

Two plural nouns joined by *or* take a plural verb:

Usually the class presidents or vice presidents sit on stage.

What happens when a sentence has two subjects, one singular and one plural, joined by *or*? In that case, the verb agrees with the *nearer* subject:

The vice presidents or the <u>president sits</u> next to the guest speakers.

but

The president or the <u>vice presidents sit</u> next to the guest speakers.

The same rule applies with two subjects joined by *either/or* and *neither/nor:* The verb agrees with the nearer subject:

Either the coach or the <u>co-captains unfurl</u> the flag.

but

Either the co-captains or <u>the coach unfurls</u> the flag.

PRACTICE 6

Complete the following sentences using a correct singular or plural verb form.

1. Neither Heidi nor her pals _____.
2. Cash or credit cards _____.
3. Either the drummer or the guitarists _____.
4. Two sweaters or one coat _____.
5. Either chocolate or butterscotch _____.

PRACTICE 7

Underline the correct verb in parentheses in the following sentences.

1. Her limpid blue eyes and golden hair (have, has) enormous appeal.
2. Wages and salaries (are, is) the same thing.
3. Chocolate chip cookies and ice cream (is, are) a favorite dessert of Flora's.
4. A solid education and a strong character (was, were) required of all applicants.
5. My parents and my boyfriend (urges, urge) me to finish college.

The Indefinite Pronouns *Each, Everyone, Anybody, Somebody,* and *Nobody*

Indefinite pronouns are so called because they refer to no specific—or *definite*—person. The following indefinite pronouns always take a singular verb:

another	everyone	nothing
anybody	everything	one

anything	nobody	somebody
anyone	none	
everybody	no one	

Here are some examples:

Everybody <u>has</u> (not *have*) the duty to protect our freedoms.

Everyone <u>opposes</u> (not *oppose*) the new mall.

Nobody <u>wishes</u> (not *wish*) him more luck and happiness than we do.

Another <u>makes</u> (not *make*) a different point entirely.

USAGE MONITOR

none

For a long time, English experts argued about whether the word *none* is plural or singular. The general agreement today is that it can be both, depending on what is emphasized:

None dares (singular) or *dare* (plural) call it treason.

Almost *none* of the soldiers *were* wounded.

Since *none* is followed by *of the soldiers,* the plural is preferred.

PRACTICE 8

Underline the correct verb in parentheses.

1. Anyone in this room (has, have) the right to vote.

2. Everyone (has, have) a mind with which to decide.

3. One of the paramedics (comes, come) from Guadalajara.

4. Somebody (is, are) hiding behind that bush.

5. None of the restaurants (is, are) open.

Who, Which, and *That*

USAGE MONITOR

Who or *whom*? That is the question. Those of us who love old-fashioned grammar are sad to notice the death of the pronoun *whom*. While grammar books and dictionaries continue to distinguish between *who* as a subject ("*who* is knocking at the door?") and *whom* as an object ("*whom* did you kick?"), headlines in respectable newspapers now write, "*Who* should the government hold responsible?" or, "Man seeks revenge on those *who* he hates." Granted, complex sentences such as "*Who* do you think is the best quarterback?" require careful thought to figure out that *who* is the subject of the verb *is,* not *whom,* the object of the verb *think*. The world at large may use *who* as the all-purpose relative pronoun, but the proper distinction between *who* and *whom* remains a stamp of educated writing. In informal writing, *who* is acceptable for both the subject and object:

> *Who* drove you home? (Subject)
>
>   and
>
> *Who* do you prefer? (Object)

Who, which, and *that* are often used to replace nouns in dependent clauses. When they are so used, they should agree with the *closest* preceding noun. An example follows.

Incorrect: My mother is one of the reporters who covers City Hall.

Correct: My mother is one of the reporters who cover City Hall.

The closest noun that comes before *who* is not *mother* but *reporters*. It is *reporters* that therefore determines the case of the verb.

In fact, the sentence is a blend of two smaller sentences:

> My mother is one of the reporters. The reporters cover City Hall.

The *who* stands for *reporters*, not for *mother*.

Here are other examples:

Leon or Ray is one of the climbers who <u>are</u> going to attempt the pinnacle.	(*climbers*, not *Leon* or *Ray*, is the closest noun before *who*)
Among my greatest fears and worries <u>is</u> encountering a snake that spits poison.	(*snake*, not *fears* or *worries*, is the closest noun before *that*)

PRACTICE 9

Circle the closest noun preceding *who, which,* or *that* in the following sentences. Then underline the correct verb.

1. She is among those scientists who (believe, believes) in Martians.

2. Fabio is one of several students who (merit, merits) an award.

3. The barn is one of the buildings that (need, needs) painting.

4. Patsy is among the seniors who (is, are) dissatisfied.

5. The trunk and suitcases, which (look, looks) sturdy, fall apart easily.

Error 3 Review

The following paragraph contains subject–verb agreement errors. Rewrite the paragraph, making all required corrections.

> One of my strongest wishes are to have a flower garden filled with roses, pansies, sweet peas, and other colorful blossoms. But no one

realize more than I do that tending a flower garden is constant work. Once you decides to plant a flower garden, you have to take care of it regularly. You has to pull out the weeds that quickly grows, and you has to water regularly. It don't matter if you are tired and prefer watching TV; the garden call you when it need tending. There's the various weather problems to consider as well. For instance, a hot sun or strong winds ruins flowers. A heavy, pelting rain destroys blooms, too. Children and animals is another problem. They has little awareness of flowers and will trample them as they runs or plays. Aunt Bee is among my relatives who has a spectacular flower garden. Either she or her two sons works in it every single day to keep it beautiful. Nobody know better than they how much work a garden takes. Until I am sure that I have plenty of time to devote to a flower garden, I guess I'll just enjoy gardens that has been grown by my friends and relatives.

 To check your progress in meeting this chapter's objectives, log in to **www.mywritinglab.com,** go to the **Study Plan** tab, click on **The 20 Most Common Sentence Errors** and choose **Subject-Verb Agreement** from the list of subtopics. Read and view the resources in the **Review Materials** section, and then complete the **Recall, Apply,** and **Write** sets in the **Activities** section.

ERROR 4

INCORRECT VERB FORMS

GRAMMARIAN

WOOF
WOOFS
WOOFING
WOOFED

www.CartoonStock.com

s. harris

Learning Objective

- Define regular verbs, irregular verbs, helping verbs, and problem verbs in the present, past, and past participle tenses.

Verbs are either regular or irregular. Regular verbs form the past tense by adding *-d* or *-ed*. They also form the past participle by adding *-d* or *-ed*. The past participle generally refers to actions in the distant, rather than in the immediate, past. It requires a helping verb, either *have, has,* or *had.* Here are some examples of common regular verbs:

PRESENT TENSE	PAST TENSE	PAST PARTICIPLE
charge	charged	have, has, *or* had charged
live	lived	have, has, *or* had lived
bake	baked	have, has, *or* had baked
hike	hiked	have, has, *or* had hiked
heave	heaved	have, has, *or* had heaved

Here are some examples of these words in sentences:

Past:	He lived in California for a year.
Past participle:	He has lived in some exotic places.
	He had lived in New York many years ago.
Past:	They baked the cake yesterday.
Past participle:	They have baked many cakes.
	They had already baked the birthday cake.

Don't let your ear fool you into dropping the *-d* or *-ed* endings of past tense verbs. Although this is a mistake we all occasionally make in everyday speech, you must not make it in your writing.

Dropped ending:	They were suppose to do better.
	They were not use to the heat.
Correct:	They were supposed to do better.
	They were not used to the heat.

PRACTICE 1

Change the underlined regular verb in each sentence to the past participle. Remember to use *has, have,* or *had.* Write out the entire sentence.

1. They <u>decide</u> not to go.

_____

2. Maxine <u>bought</u> a new computer.

_____

3. Her mother <u>worked</u> as my father's accountant.

_____

4. The dog <u>sniffs</u> at the fire hydrant.

_____

5. We <u>row</u> every day on the lake.

_____

Omitting the Helping Verb from a Past Participle

In some slangy talk, it is common to drop the helping verb in a past participle—a usage your ear might even excuse. However, dropping the helping verb, whether your ear approves or not, is *always* wrong in writing. Here are some examples:

Dropped verb:	I seen that movie.
Written form:	I <u>have</u> seen that movie.
Dropped verb:	We been around the block twice.
Written form:	We <u>have</u> been around the block twice.
Dropped verb:	Why Harry brought flowers?
Written form:	Why <u>has</u> Harry brought flowers?

USAGE MONITOR

can, may

Don't confuse these two words because they are not interchangeable. *Can* expresses ability or knowledge, as in

> Fumiko *can* lift a huge rock by himself.

or

> Suzy *can* multiply large numbers in her head.

On the other hand, *may* expresses possibility or permission, as in

> *May* I have the butter, please?

or

> Tomorrow we *may* play soccer.

PRACTICE 2

Rewrite each sentence below in the lines provided, inserting the helping verb where it belongs.

1. He been a cocky kid since he was young.

_____

2. She said she given enough for one day.

_____

3. The refrigerator frozen the food.

_____

4. You eaten yet?

_____

5. They fallen from a high place.

_____

PRACTICE 3

The paragraph that follows contains errors in the use of past participles. First underline each error; second, rewrite the paragraph with the correct past participles.

My budget fallen on hard times lately. No matter how hard I try, it been really hard to make ends meet. If I work a full shift, I clear

$120 per week. Last year this use to be enough to pay my bills, but this year it isn't. It costs me about $60 per week for rent. That leaves me with about half of what I take home. For food, I use to budget $20 per week, but this year for some reason, that simply isn't enough. I'm more likely to spend at least $30 for food, and that means eating a lot of junk. Last year I could occasionally go out for a hamburger, but not this year. So after rent and food, I have about $30 left for everything else. I'm suppose to pay car insurance and tuition and everything with that amount. That means, if I want to go to movie, which costs about $7, or nearly a third of my weekly pay that's left, I really have to think hard. I ask myself, what could happened that I'm so broke this year? I think it's because everything gone up. What used to cost $5 last year now costs about $7. Gasoline gone up, too, and it seems I'm buying more gas. Maybe my car become a gas guzzler. I don't know. All I know is that I can barely make ends meet.

_____

_____

_____

_____

_____

_____

_____

_____

_____

_____

_____

_____

Irregular verbs

Verbs are **irregular** if their past tense is not formed by adding *-d* or *-ed*. For example, if the rule for changing tenses were applied to *bring,* its past tense would be *bringed.* But it isn't—it's *brought. Bring* is therefore an irregular verb.

Below is a list of irregular verbs that many of us use every day. Remember, the past participle always requires the use of the helping verb *have, has,* or *had.*

SOME COMMON IRREGULAR VERBS

PRESENT	PAST	PAST PARTICIPLE
arise	arose	arisen
be	was	been
bear	bore	borne

become	became	become
begin	began	begun
break	broke	broken
bring	brought (not *brung*)	brought
build	built	built
burst	burst (not *busted*)	burst
buy	bought	bought
catch	caught	caught
choose	chose	chosen
cling	clung	clung
come	came	come
dive	dove	dived
do	did (not *done*)	done
draw	drew	drawn
drink	drank	drunk
drive	drove	driven
eat	ate	eaten
fall	fell	fallen
feed	fed	fed
feel	felt	felt
fight	fought	fought
fly	flew	flown
forgive	forgave	forgiven
freeze	froze	frozen
get	got	gotten
go	went	gone
grow	grew	grown
hang (*clothes*)	hung	hung
hang (*execute*)	hanged	hanged
have	had	had
hold	held	held
hurt	hurt (not *hurted*)	hurt
know	knew	known
lay	laid	laid
lead	led	led
lie	lay	lain
lose	lost	lost
make	made	made
mean	meant	meant
meet	met	met
pay	paid	paid

(*continued*)

PRESENT	PAST	PAST PARTICIPLE
put	put	put
read	read	read
ride	rode	ridden
ring	rang	rung
rise	rose	risen
run	ran	run
say	said	said
see	saw (not *seen*)	seen
seek	sought (not *seeked*)	sought
sell	sold	sold
set	set	set
shake	shook	shaken
shine	shone	shone
shrink	shrank	shrunk
sing	sang	sung
sink	sank	sunk
sleep	slept	slept
speak	spoke	spoken
spend	spent	spent
spin	spun	spun
spit	spat	spat
spring	sprang (not *sprung*)	sprung
stand	stood	stood
steal	stole	stolen
sting	stung	stung
stink	stank (not *stunk*)	stunk
strike	struck	struck
strive	strove	striven
swear	swore	sworn
swim	swam (not *swum*)	swum
swing	swung	swung
take	took	taken
teach	taught	taught
tear	tore	torn
tell	told	told
think	thought	thought
throw	threw	thrown
understand	understood	understood
wake	woke	woken
wear	wore	worn

weave	wove	woven
win	won	won
wring	wrung	wrung
write	wrote	written

USAGE MONITOR

sneak

For some reason, most people think that this verb is irregular even though it is regular. Even well-known TV commentators will say something like this: "The thief *snuck* into the house." This is grammatically wrong and should be "The thief *sneaked* into the house." Just convince yourself that "snuck" simply doesn't exist. The past tense of *sneak* is *sneaked*. Tell your friends, too.

PRACTICE 4

Complete the following chart. Refer to the list of irregular verbs beginning on page 84 if in doubt.

PRESENT	PAST	PAST PARTICIPLE
1. seek		
2. sell		
3. steal		
4. ring		
5. fly		
6. teach		
7. hurt		
8. strive		
9. hang (*execute*)		
10. spit		

PRACTICE 5

In the following sentences, the past tense is used incorrectly. Write the correct form in the spaces provided.

1. _____ His mother <u>waked</u> him up to go to work.

2. _____ She <u>weared</u> that blouse yesterday.

3. _____ I <u>throwed</u> the ball to the pitcher.

4. _____ They <u>selled</u> themselves short.

5. _____ I could have <u>ate</u> the whole cake.

6. _____ The worker <u>striked</u> for better pay.

7. _____ I've <u>fighted</u> that battle before.

8. _____ Because of the yeast, the bread had <u>raised</u>.

9. _____ I found out I <u>payed</u> too much for the battery.

10. _____ She <u>swinged</u> in the park all morning.

USAGE MONITOR

choose, chose

The rule for correct usage is simple: *Choose* is the present tense; *chose* is the past tense.

Here are two examples, with *choose/chose* used correctly:

Sooner or later, we all *choose* the foods we like.

but

Petro *chose* to serve in the Iraq War.

The different pronunciation should help you decide which word is correct.

Problems with Irregular Verbs

Two problems are common with the everyday use of irregular verbs:

* Using the simple past instead of the past participle:

| **Incorrect:** | She has wove two rugs. |
| **Correct:** | She has woven two rugs. |

| **Incorrect:** | They have tore the book. |
| **Correct:** | They have torn the book. |

* Using an incorrect form of the past participle:

| **Incorrect:** | He had brung his Rollerblades to school before. |
| **Correct:** | He had brought his Rollerblades to school before. |

| **Incorrect:** | She has broke the remote control. |
| **Correct:** | She has broken the remote control. |

Beware of these two common errors.

PRACTICE 6

Some of the underlined past participles that follow are correct, and some are incorrect. If the participle is correct, write *C* in the blank; if it is incorrect, write the correct participle in the blank.

1. _____ I have <u>wore</u> that many times.

2. _____ They couldn't have <u>sang</u> any worse.

3. _____ The president has <u>saw</u> to the problem.

4. _____ They have <u>drug</u> the boat through the mud flat.

5. _____ Because of the freezing weather, the pipes have <u>busted</u>.

6. _____ In another move or two, he will have <u>sprang</u> the trap.

7. _____ Because she washed my jeans in water that was too hot, they have <u>shrunk</u>.

8. _____ She has <u>wrote</u> him three times.

9. _____ I have <u>drew</u> my own conclusions.

10. _____ You have <u>ran</u> away from home for the last time.

Problem Verbs

A few verbs seem to give the entire English-speaking world trouble. They are *lie/lay, sit/set,* and *rise/raise.*

Lie/lay

Here are the principal parts of these two verbs:

PRESENT	PAST	PAST PARTICIPLE
lie	lay	lain = to rest in a horizontal position as when sleeping
lay	laid	laid = to set down something—for instance, a book

TO LIE (WHO?)	TO LAY (WHAT?)
I like to lie on the grass.	She lays the tile in the bathroom.
The dog is lying on the grass.	She is laying the tile in the bathroom.
Yesterday I lay on the grass.	Yesterday she laid the tile in the bathroom.
I have lain on the grass too long.	She must have laid the tile in the bathroom.

PRACTICE 7

Underline the correct verb in parentheses.

1. (Lie, Lay) the portable phone on the desk.

2. I have been (lying, laying) plans in my dreams.

3. He was (lain, laid) to rest with all military honors.

4. She was tired and went to (lie, lay) down.

5. She complains that all he does is (lie, lay) around watching television.

Sit/set

Here are the principal parts of *sit* and *set:*

PRESENT	PAST	PAST PARTICIPLE
sit	sat	sat = to rest on one's bottom
set	set	set = to place something somewhere

TO SIT (WHO?)	TO SET (WHAT?)
He sits at the head of the table.	The child sets his toys by his bed.
She is sitting by the window.	He is setting the toys in a row.
The crew sat in the cockpit.	Last night he set the bear next to the giraffe.
They have always sat in the front row.	Did he set the toys on the table?

PRACTICE 8

Underline the correct verb in parentheses.

1. They (sat, set) in the bleachers, hoping to catch a fly ball.

2. I'm (sitting, setting) the groceries on the counter.

3. (Sit, Set) yourself down on the sofa and listen to me play the piano.

4. She (sat, set) the socket wrench set on the bench.

5. (Sit, Set) with me under the tree and listen to the bird sing.

Rise/raise

Here are the principal parts of *rise* and *raise:*

PRESENT	PAST	PAST PARTICIPLE
rise	rose	risen = to get up or move up on your own
raise	raised	raised = to lift up someone or something

TO RISE (WHO?)	TO RAISE (WHAT?)
Let us rise and be counted.	You should not raise your hopes too much.
I am rising early to greet the dawn.	She is raising the hem two inches.
Everyone rose when the anthem was played.	They raised the flag.
The audience has risen.	She has raised an objection.

PRACTICE 9

Change the underlined word(s) by substituting the correct form of *rise* or *raise*. Do not change the tense of the original.

1. _____ <u>Lift</u> the banner above your head.

2. _____ The moon <u>came</u> up over the ocean.

3. _____ The entire team had <u>stood up</u> to watch the home run.

4. _____ Victory <u>pulled up</u> their spirits.

5. _____ He <u>got up</u> late today.

Lie/lay, sit/set, rise/raise: **Does it really matter?**

Even if students don't ask the question "Does it really matter if I say *lie* or *lay*?", they often think it. The answer is, yes, it does matter.

True, if you commanded, "Lay down!" instead of "Lie down!", your dog would probably obey just as quickly. "If I'm understood when I incorrectly say *lay* instead of *lie,* or *lie* instead of *lay,* why does using the correct form matter?" is what many students wonder. Being understood, however, is no substitute for being correct. Furthermore, being correct is what makes you understandable.

Language does change, and as the years roll by, we predict that one day, *lie* and *lay* will have the same meaning in grammar books. Until that day comes, however, their differences do matter. For example, you might scribble this memo to your boss: "Dear Boss, I lay the contract on your desk before I left." Upon reading it, your boss might mutter, "No, you didn't. You <u>laid</u> it there. If you can't get that right, how can I trust you with this important contract? I'm giving the account to Nancy instead." In other words, these little differences are important because they matter to other people.

Of course, they don't matter if you work for a dog.

Error 4 Review

The paragraph below contains errors in the past tense and past participles of irregular verbs. Find and correct all the errors.

When I began working at Gary's Restaurant, I was lead to believe that I would soon be given a rise in pay. Mrs. Smith, my supervisor, even complimented me when I was hired, telling me that I brung a lot of experience to the company. Now as I set here writing this letter, I cannot help but feel that I was misleaded. I don't want to rise this point and belabor it, but when the pipes in the kitchen busted, I was the one who saved the food in the walk-in. Furthermore, in my six months of employment here, I have never shrinked from doing my duty. Whatever my supervisor told me to do, I always did it as well as I understanded the request. Nobody has ever wringed work out of me. I'm always the first to volunteer. I have wrote this letter because I feel not only mistreated, but also misleaded. . . . As I drived to work my first few months on the job, I thought to myself that Gary's is a good place to work. But now my confidence has been shook. Now that I have spoke my honest opinion, I hope that I will get the pay increase I deserve. I hope by this letter I have not fell out of favor. But I was brung up to believe honesty is the best policy.

 To check your progress in meeting this chapter's objectives, log in to **www.mywritinglab.com,** go to the **Study Plan** tab, click on **The 20 Most Common Sentence Errors** and choose **Regular and Irregular Verbs** from the list of subtopics. Read and view the resources in the **Review Materials** section, and then complete the **Recall, Apply,** and **Write** sets in the **Activities** section.

ERROR

5 INCORRECT FORMS OF *DO, BE,* AND *HAVE*

Even if you've spoken English all your life, verbs can still be troublesome. Part of the problem is that we don't speak and write verbs the same way. In speech we sometimes drop the tense endings of verbs when we shouldn't, as in this sentence:

> She laugh all the time.

Or, we add an ending when we shouldn't:

> They laughs all the time.

In the first sentence, since *She* is singular, the verb must also be singular—*laughs*. In the second sentence, since *They* is plural, the verb must also be plural—*laugh*.

You can make these mistakes in everyday speech—we all occasionally do—and be forgiven. You should not, however, make them in writing. The standards for grammar are stricter in writing than in speech, meaning that you must always write verb tenses correctly.

Learning Objective

- Understand the correct forms of *do, be,* and *have* in the present and past tense as well as with verbs ending in *–ing*

Present Tense Endings

In standard English you must use the correct endings with verbs. You cannot use a plural ending with a singular subject, or a singular ending with a plural subject. Here are the correct endings for regular verbs in the present tense:

PRESENT TENSE—SINGULAR

INCORRECT	CORRECT
I walks	I walk
You walks	You walk
He, she, it walk	He, she, it walks

93

PRESENT TENSE—PLURAL

INCORRECT	CORRECT
We walks	We walk
You walks	You walk
They walks	They walk

Present tense problems

There are two kinds of problems that commonly occur with verbs in the present tense:

- Dropped -s/-es endings for *he, she,* and *it.*

Incorrect:	He take the train to work.
Correct:	He takes the train to work.

Incorrect:	She make pancakes for breakfast.
Correct:	She makes pancakes for breakfast.

Incorrect:	It drive me crazy when she act like that.
Correct:	It drives me crazy when she acts like that.

- Unnecessary -s/-es for *we, you,* and *they.*

Incorrect:	We visits Gram every weekend.
Correct:	We visit Gram every weekend.

Incorrect:	You always smiles, even in sad times.
Correct:	You always smile, even in sad times.

Incorrect:	They both plays the accordion.
Correct:	They both play the accordion.

USAGE MONITOR

Problems with dropped and added endings occur, as we said, because we are less precise in our speech than we must be in our writing. If you make such errors regularly in your speech, your ear may not be particularly helpful in catching them. In that case, you should simply memorize the correct endings and practice them the way guitarists practice the guitar.

PRACTICE 1

In the blanks provided, write *C* if the verb is correct and *NC* if it is not.

1. ____ Bernice and I drives in the same car pool.

2. ____ We try to pay our electricity bill.

3. ____ Our neighbor keep trying to win the lottery.

4. ____Jeremy buy Melinda's affection.

5. ____ She repeat herself constantly.

6. ____ Fran ignored the "No U-Turn" sign.

7. ____ They keep wearing ugly hats.

8. ____ My mom and I sticks to our opinion.

9. ____ It bothers me when they fight.

10. ____ They constantly eats fattening foods.

PRACTICE 2

In the passage that follows, strike out any incorrect verb and write the correct form above it.

Most of my friends likes to watch soccer. During the World Cup season, we sits in front of my TV all day long to watch the competition. My friend Danny always support the team from Brazil, but I cheer for the Italian team with Baggio, who wear a braid down his back. That seem cool to me. The penalty kicks excites everyone the most. Then we screams and yells at the top of our voices. If the kicker make a goal, we goes crazy. If the goalie intercept the ball, we explodes. Soccer get you involved, no matter what side win.

Past Tense Endings

Here are the correct endings for regular singular verbs in the past tense:

PAST TENSE—SINGULAR

INCORRECT	CORRECT
I walk	I walked
You walk	You walked
He, she, it walk	He, she, it walked

Here are the correct endings for regular plural verbs in the past tense:

PAST TENSE—PLURAL

INCORRECT	CORRECT
We walk	We walked
You walk	You walked
They walk	They walked

With both singular and plural verbs, we can be careless in our speech and drop the *-ed* ending. In writing, however, you must *always* use the *-ed* ending with regular verbs in the past tense.

Incorrect:	I pick up the mail yesterday.
Correct:	I picked up the mail yesterday.
Incorrect:	He drop several hints.
Correct:	He dropped several hints.

PRACTICE 3

In the blank at the beginning of each sentence, write the past tense of the underlined verb.

1. _____ The mechanical teddy bear <u>dance</u> a jig.

2. _____ Studies <u>suggest</u> that TV violence is bad.

3. _____ Despite my pleadings, Betty <u>continue</u> to smoke.

4. _____ Some countries <u>remain</u> neutral during the war.

5. _____ He <u>manage</u> to turn the tiny argument into a major problem.

6. _____ Beverly <u>challenge</u> her opponent.

7. _____ Jack and Jill <u>decide</u> to go up the hill.

8. _____ I secretly <u>open</u> the door to the safe.

9. _____ The strange voice on the telephone <u>ask</u> my name.

10. _____ They <u>litter</u> the grass with cans and wrappers.

Problems with *-ing* verbs

Verbs ending in *-ing* describe an action that either is happening now or is ongoing. All *-ing* verbs need a helping verb.

> He is eating in the kitchen.
>
> He was eating in the kitchen.
>
> He has been eating in the kitchen.
>
> He had been eating in the kitchen, but now he eats in the dining room.

Two kinds of problems can occur with *-ing* verbs:

- *Be* or *been* is used instead of the correct helping verb:

Incorrect:	She be eating in the kitchen.
Correct:	She is eating in the kitchen.

or

She has been eating in the kitchen.

Incorrect:	She been studying in the library.
Correct:	She was studying in the library.
	or
	She has been studying in the library.

- The helping verb is completely omitted:

Incorrect:	They bragging too much.
Correct:	They are bragging too much.
	They were bragging too much.
	They have been bragging too much.
	They had been bragging too much.

PRACTICE 4

Rewrite the following sentences to correct the misuse of *be* or *been,* or to insert the missing helping verb.

Example: The birds be chirping outside my window.

<u>The birds are chirping outside my window.</u>

1. My car be needing a lube job.

   _____

2. She forcing her son to give up college.

   _____

3. My father buying a house near the train station.

   _____

4. How your mother be coming along with her knitting?

   _____

5. Marcy hoping she can marry next year.

   _____

6. They be ignoring all of his advice.

   _____

7. Margaret sitting under an elm tree when the lightning struck.

   _____

8. Every young person be searching for a way to feel important.

   _____

9. Dylan expecting to inherit some money from an uncle.

   _____

10. Schwarz be waiting for him in the adjoining room.

    _____

Difficult Verbs

Verbs can be hard to master. Few are harder than the three verbs we probably use more than any others in the language: *be, have,* and *do.*

To be

To be is commonly used both as a verb on its own and as a helping verb. Here is a listing of the forms of the verb *to be:*

PRESENT TENSE—SINGULAR *TO BE*

INCORRECT	CORRECT
I be, I ain't	I am, I am not
You be, you ain't	You are, you are not
He, she, it be; he, she, it ain't	He, she, it is; he, she, it is not

PRESENT TENSE—PLURAL *TO BE*

INCORRECT	CORRECT
We be, we ain't	We are, we are not
You be, you ain't	You are, you are not
They be, they ain't	They are, they are not

PAST TENSE—SINGULAR *TO BE*

INCORRECT	CORRECT
I were	I was
You was	You were
He, she, it were	He, she, it was

PAST TENSE—PLURAL *TO BE*

INCORRECT	CORRECT
We was	We were
You was	You were
They was	They were

As you can see—indeed, as you already know from repeated use—*to be* is an irregular verb. As both a verb and a helping verb, it is often incorrectly spoken. All of the sentences below, for example, are wrong, even if your ear tells you otherwise.

I ain't staying in New York.

The lake be dangerous because the wind be blowing hard.

You was rude to step in front of her.

If these are forms that you commonly use in your daily speech, be especially careful not to trust your ear with *to be*. Instead, you should memorize its correct forms.

Here is how these sentences should be written:

> I am not staying in New York.

> The lake is dangerous because the wind is blowing hard.

> You were rude to step in front of her.

PRACTICE 5

The following passage contains several errors in the use of the verb *to be*. In the space provided, rewrite the passage, correcting all errors. (*Hint:* You should find eight errors.)

> Today I be sad. It be the third anniversary of my dad's death. Believe me, even after three years, it ain't easy to lose your dad. He been my best friend. We went fishing and camping together every year. We was simply best buddies. Last summer I hiked where my dad and I had hiked along a lake high up in the Sierras. I be feeling sick with my heavy heart. My mom tried to comfort me by reminding me that I have some great memories. But that can't make up for the present loss. Right now, I wish he and I was sitting down to plan one of our famous outings. But it can't happen. He be gone forever.

To have

To have, like *to be,* is commonly used both as a verb and as a helping verb. Also like *to be,* it is an irregular verb. Here are its main forms:

PRESENT TENSE—SINGULAR *TO HAVE*

INCORRECT	CORRECT
I has	I have
You has	You have
He, she, it have	He, she, it has

PRESENT TENSE—PLURAL *TO HAVE*

INCORRECT	CORRECT
We has	We have
You has	You have
They has	They have

PAST TENSE—SINGULAR *TO HAVE*

INCORRECT	CORRECT
I has	I had
You has	You had
He, she, it have	He, she, it had

PAST TENSE—PLURAL *TO HAVE*

INCORRECT	CORRECT
We has	We had
You has	You had
They has	They had

To have is so often misused in daily speech that you should be cautious about trusting your ear to judge its correctness. The sentences below, for example, are all incorrect:

She have two nieces and two nephews.

Benny have a nifty new Honda convertible.

They has a party yesterday.

Here are the correct forms:

She has two nieces and two nephews.

Benny has a new Honda convertible.

They had a party yesterday.

PRACTICE 6

Fill in the correct form of the verb *to have* in the following sentences.

Example: She <u>has</u> to be on time.

1. Judith ____ a free ticket to the game.

2. You ____ to take him to the bus.

3. The Baxters —— two beautiful daughters.

4. He ___ my raincoat, and I must ___ it tomorrow.

5. I ___ got to live alone, and Mother ___ to understand why.

6. ___ they mentioned the problem?

7. Where ___ Pete been?

8. She ___ embarrassed me too often.

9. Everyone ___ to follow the regulations.

10. We ___ two computers, but our neighbors ___ only one.

USAGE MONITOR

have, got

Got is the past tense of *get* and should not be used in place of *have.* Similarly, *got to* should never replace *must.* The following two sentences are both wrong. Scrutinize them to make sure you understand the correct version and use it consistently:

Incorrect:	Do you *got* enough milk for the cereal?
Correct:	Do you have enough milk for the cereal?
Incorrect:	Bev *got to* catch the bus soon.
Correct:	Bev *must* catch the bus soon.

To do

The verb *to do,* like *to be* and *to have,* is used both as a verb and as a helping verb. Here are its correct forms:

PRESENT TENSE—SINGULAR *TO DO*

INCORRECT	CORRECT
I does	I do
You does	You do
He, she, it do	He, she, it does

PRESENT TENSE—PLURAL *TO DO*

INCORRECT	CORRECT
We does	We do
You does	You do
They does	They do

PAST TENSE—SINGULAR *TO DO*

INCORRECT	CORRECT
I done	I did
You done	You did
He, she, it done	He, she, it did

PAST TENSE—PLURAL *TO DO*

INCORRECT	CORRECT
We done	We did
You done	You did
They done	They did

The main problem with *to do* is that it is used in informal speech differently than how it is used in writing. So, again, do not trust your ear. All the sentences below, for example, are incorrect:

He don't have the sense to come in out of the rain.

I does whatever I'm told.

She done her homework early.

Here are the correct forms:

He doesn't have the sense to come in out of the rain.

I do whatever I'm told.

She did her homework early.

or

She has done her homework early.

PRACTICE 7

Use the correct form of *to do* in the following sentences.

1. He _____ admire his parents' high standards.

2. She _____ whine considerably, _____ she?

3. _____ you belong to a study group?

4. How _____ you get the wallpaper off the wall?

5. Melissa rarely _____ poorly on math exams.

6. I _____ object to his superior attitude.

7. _____ Mr. Smith understand that the payment is due today?

8. Where _____ they dispose of their trash?

9. _____ not interfere in our argument.

10. _____ it matter whether or not he believes you?

Error 5 Review

Fill in the blanks with the correct form of the verb in parentheses.

1. Yesterday, Julie (insist) _____ that we go with her.

2. Melvin (be) _____ the grump of the year.

3. They both (be) _____ good readers.

4. Last May, Elvira (decide) _____ to buy a blond wig.

5. Miranda (do) _____ follow him around too much.

6. David still (eat) _____ too many sweets.

7. She (hide) _____ her spy novels so that I can't get them.

8. If you (be) _____ satisfied, then pay the workmen.

9. The roof (have) _____ a terrible leak.

10. (Do) _____ she always tease you so unmercifully?

11. Jessie (have) _____ told us some crazy gossip.

12. City Hall (have) _____ the duty to build safe bridges.

13. If she (swim) _____ to the island, she (be) _____ strong.

14. You have (do) _____ the most work.

15. The door (have) _____ to be sanded down and painted.

The paragraph that follows contains incorrect forms of the *be, have,* and *do* verbs. Rewrite the paragraph to correct these errors. (*Hint:* You should be able to find 21 errors.)

If I be a waitress, I would try to be cheerful, efficient, and polite. So many waitresses nowadays doesn't offer good service. If I be a waitress, I would approach the customer with a smile and a warm greeting. I wouldn't just grab my notebook and ask, "What would you like to order?" The other day at Benny's coffee shop, where my best friend and I be going for breakfast, the waitress at our table ask us abruptly, "What can I get you?" I be surprised by such a cold attitude, and my friend have a hard time giving her order for pancakes. After she be taking our order, the waitress walk over to another customer and talk, talk, talk without even placing our order with the kitchen. I be really offended. We was in a hurry, and this waitress deliberately ignore our needs. Well, finally she brought our order, but when she place it on the table, she spill some coffee and made noise banging the dishes because she be so rough. Most polite waitresses wish you a pleasant meal or tell you to "enjoy," but not this one. She just disappear until we call her over to get our check. I have no idea why she do her job so poorly. If I be a waitress, I be trying hard to please my customers.

_____

_____

_____

_____

_____

_____

_____

_____

_____

_____

To check your progress in meeting this chapter's objectives, log in to **www.mywritinglab.com,** go to the **Study Plan** tab, click on **The 20 Most Common Sentence Errors** and choose **Verbs** from the list of subtopics. Read and view the resources in the **Review Materials** section, and then complete the **Recall, Apply,** and **Write** sets in the **Activities** section.

ERROR
6 PASSIVE VOICE

English has two voices: the active and the passive voice. The **active voice** stresses *who* did an act. The **passive voice** stresses *to whom* or *to what* an act was done. Most of us usually speak in the active voice because it is simpler and more direct.

Learning Objective

- Explain the difference between active and passive voice.

> **Active voice:**   The cashier gave us our change.
>
> **Passive voice:**   Our change was given to us by the cashier.

Writers who wish to avoid naming names often prefer the passive voice because it can be used to hide the doer. Here is a case in point.

> The tax return was lost.

Who lost the tax return? The active voice would have told us:

> Bill lost the tax return.

USAGE MONITOR

If you have trouble seeing the difference between the *active voice* and the *passive voice,* here's an image to help you: Joe is a teaser, and he loves to pinch Bernice, his younger sister, who is frail and never resists. He does the pinching, so he represents the *active voice.* Bernice doesn't resist, sitting quietly and getting pinched by Joe, so she represents the *passive voice.*

In writing you should mainly use the active voice. It is livelier and stronger than the passive voice and more like everyday talk. The passive voice is occasionally used in scientific reporting, where what was done is more important than which researcher did it:

> The chemical mixture was heated.

It is also occasionally used in instances where an effect is more important than its cause:

> The fishing village was destroyed by a tidal wave.

Here the important fact is the destruction of the village. That it was destroyed by a tidal wave is secondary.

105

PRACTICE 1

Read the paired sentences aloud and write *A* in the blank beside the sentence in the active voice.

Example: __*A*__ **(a).** Louise made the coffee.

_____ **(b).** The coffee was made by Louise.

1. _____ **(a).** The package was advertised by the travel agent.

_____ **(b).** The travel agent advertised the package.

2. _____ **(a).** Initiative is crushed by bureaucracy.

_____ **(b).** Bureaucracy crushes initiative.

3. _____ **(a).** Mrs. Stanhope spoke to the letter carrier.

_____ **(b).** The letter carrier was spoken to by Mrs. Stanhope.

4. _____ **(a).** The people were misled by the cult.

_____ **(b).** The cult misled the people.

5. _____ **(a).** The boat was stopped by the Coast Guard.

_____ **(b).** The Coast Guard stopped the boat.

6. _____ **(a).** I enjoyed the lecture.

_____ **(b).** The lecture was enjoyed by me.

7. _____ **(a).** The play was staged by the Drama Club.

_____ **(b).** The Drama Club staged the play.

8. _____ **(a).** An invasion of ants interrupted the picnic.

_____ **(b).** The picnic was interrupted by an invasion of ants.

9. _____ **(a).** The developer obtained the building permit.

_____ **(b).** The building permit was obtained by the developer.

10. _____ **(a).** A strong case was made by the prosecuting attorney.

_____ **(b).** The prosecuting attorney made a strong case.

PRACTICE 2

Rewrite the sentences below to change verbs to the active voice from the passive voice.

Example: The marshmallows were enjoyed by the Boy Scouts.

Answer: The Boy Scouts enjoyed the marshmallows.

1. An ace was served by the tennis champion.

_____

2. The home was inspected by the building inspector.

_____

3. The movie was enjoyed by everyone.

   _____

4. The sugar water was relished by the hummingbirds.

   _____

5. A screenplay was written by my neighbor.

   _____

6. The candidate was backed by women's groups.

   _____

7. Jogging is done by many people for exercise.

   _____

8. The statue was removed by the protesters.

   _____

9. The law was passed by the Senate.

   _____

10. The taxicab was summoned by the doorman.

    _____

PRACTICE 3

Rewrite these sentences to put them in the active voice.

1. A bad fall was suffered by the pole vaulter.

   _____

2. The car was fixed by the mechanic.

   _____

3. Encouragement was given to the class by the dean.

   _____

4. New soles were put on the shoes by the shoemaker.

   _____

5. The order was placed by Jim.

   _____

6. A standing ovation was given by the audience.

   _____

7. The plane was guided in by the air controller.

   _____

8. The poor homeowners were robbed by the slick-talking con man.

   _____

9. The wonderful tarts were made by him.

_____

10. An incentive was offered by the sales manager.

_____

11. A lively tune was played by the band.

_____

12. Our snow was shoveled by our neighbor's son.

_____

13. The oven was cleaned by me.

_____

14. The syllabus was handed out by the professor.

_____

15. A safety flare was shot off by the lifeguard.

_____

Error 6 Review

Rewrite the following paragraph in the active voice.

Last summer our house was painted by me. The job took about two weeks. First, the exterior was washed using warm water and a mild detergent. Then all the chinks and pores in the walls were sealed with putty. It was not an easy job. After the putty had had a chance to dry, the exterior could be painted. A latex paint was used because it is easy to apply and cleans up with water. A whole week was needed to finish this part of the job. I was very careful to apply the paint evenly because I did not want to have to apply two coats. A color was used that was very close to the original color. Our house is a two-story house, which meant that a ladder was needed to do the second story. This was the hardest part of the job. It meant working 35 or 40 feet high, which was not easy. The paint can had to be balanced on the top rung of the ladder while I worked. Plus it was very hot, and I had to keep going down to drink water. But when the job was finished, a great deal of satisfaction was felt by me. I had to pat myself on the back. Even my dad said that a good job was done.

_____

_____

_____

_____

_____

_____

_____

_____

_____

 To check your progress in meeting this chapter's objectives, log in to **www.mywritinglab.com,** go to the **Study Plan** tab, click on **The 20 Most Common Sentence Errors** and choose **Consistent Verb Tense and Active Voice** from the list of subtopics. Read and view the resources in the **Review Materials** section, and then complete the **Recall, Apply,** and **Write** sets in the **Activities** section.

7 SHIFTS IN TENSE

I f you begin a sentence in the present tense, you must end it in the present tense. If you begin in the past tense, you must end in the past tense. For example, look at this sentence:

> Larry blew a tire, and then just keeps on driving.

The problem with the sentence is that it begins with a verb in the past tense and ends with a verb in the present tense. Larry is made into a time-traveler—hopping from the past to the present in one breath. To be correct, the sentence must read:

> Larry blew a tire, and then   **(All past tense)**
> just kept on driving.
>
> or
>
> Larry blows a tire, and then   **(All present tense)**
> just keeps on driving.

Your tense use must be consistent. You must not shift tenses unless there is a logical reason for doing so.

Learning Objective

- Identify unnecessary shifts in tense and correct them to avoid confusing the reader

USAGE MONITOR

The rule about not shifting tense seems pretty simple. Yet, because people mix up their verb tenses all the time in everyday speech ("Yesterday I *walked* into our kitchen and—guess what—I *see* our dog chewing my cap..."), your ear might mislead you into making the same mistake in writing. Be alert to this possibility. Make sure your verbs in a written sentence all use the same tense.

PRACTICE 1

Correct the shifts in verb tense in these sentences.

1. The teacher writes the assignment on the board, and then left the room with no comment.

   _____

   _____

2. When I warned her that the road was slippery, she simply pays no attention.

   _____

   _____

3. He memorizes the entire Bill of Rights, but failed the test anyway.

   _____

   _____

4. When clouds covered the moon, the lovers leave the park.

   _____

   _____

5. I had barely started my laundry when the washing machine floods all over the floor.

   _____

   _____

6. She grabbed the pen on the desk and hurriedly signs the contract.

   _____

   _____

7. The night before her wedding, Annie had dinner with her best friends and weeps for two hours.

   _____

   _____

8. When the first snow falls, the men in the neighborhood got out their shovels to clear the walkways.

   _____

   _____

9. All of us lustily sang "I've Been Workin' on the Railroad," and then we eat three huge pizzas.

   _____

   _____

10. He climbed to the top of the hill and builds a fire.

   _____

   _____

PRACTICE 2

Correct the shifts in verb tense in these sentences.

1. Mary recognized the car and is yelling, "There goes the thief!"

_____

_____

2. For 20 years he has kept the secret and never tells a soul.

_____

_____

3. We stop recruiting volunteers and had started to work.

_____

_____

4. Tom envied Lud and wants to take over his job.

_____

_____

5. The clouds looked menacing, so we pull up our stakes and leave the camp.

_____

_____

6. I look out the window and saw three fire engines.

_____

_____

7. They paid for her tuition and gave her spending money, but she never shows an ounce of gratitude.

_____

_____

8. He is a carpenter and has received good benefits.

_____

_____

9. Although I felt dizzy, I manage to cross the stream on the rope bridge.

_____

_____

10. She's telling us an old story, but we listened with fascination.

_____

_____

PRACTICE 3

Complete the sentences below using the correct verb tense.

1. She set the table, while he _____.

2. People gathered around the accident and then the fire truck _____

   _____.

3. Before the curtain rose, the actor _____.

4. When the wind howls outside our windows, _____.

5. We made reservations for 7:00, which _____.

6. They did apologize, so _____.

7. Francis walks two miles every day, but _____.

8. They applauded the mayor and then _____.

9. December was mild, but January _____.

10. He leaves the cap off the toothpaste, and _____.

Error 7 Review

Rewrite the following paragraph to correct all shifts in tense.

My mother is so funny. Once she watched a TV program about regular car maintenance. Then, for weeks afterward, she gives our family long harangues about getting the oil changed regularly and replacing a weak battery. "Won't you feel silly if you were in a busy intersection and your car stalled?" she must have asks me every night. And practically all day Saturday, there she is in the garage, checking some hose or gasket or belt. She visited every neighbor and points out the dangers of ignoring an oil leak or bad brakes. "Watch out for uneven tire wear," she preaches to everyone. My father was embarrassed that Mom is so forward about telling our neighbors how to run their lives. He tells her that if she wanted to take good care of her car, fine, but that she should allow the neighbors to make their own decisions about their own cars.

_____

_____

_____

_____

_____

_____

_____

_____

_____

_____

_____

_____

_____

_____

mywritinglab To check your progress in meeting this chapter's objectives, log in to **www.mywritinglab.com,** go to the **Study Plan** tab, click on **The 20 Most Common Sentence Errors** and choose **Tense** from the list of subtopics. Read and view the resources in the **Review Materials** section, and then complete the **Recall, Apply,** and **Write** sets in the **Activities** section.

ERROR 8

SHIFTS IN POINT OF VIEW

Writing is easier to read if it uses the same point of view throughout. You may choose a first person, second person, or third person point of view:

	FIRST PERSON	SECOND PERSON	THIRD PERSON
SINGULAR	I	You	He, she, it, one
PLURAL	We	You	They

Learning Objectives

- Understand the three points of view: first person, second person, and third person

- Explain the importance of maintaining a single point of view

Here are some examples:

Incorrect: When <u>a person</u> sees an accident, <u>you</u> should immediately offer assistance.

Correct: When <u>you</u> see an accident, <u>you</u> should immediately offer assistance.

or

When <u>one</u> sees an accident, <u>one</u> should immediately offer assistance.

Here is a paragraph containing many shifts:

How <u>we</u> wake up in the morning affects how <u>you</u> view the rest of the day. If <u>you</u> start the day off badly, <u>we'll</u> be in a bad mood for the rest of the day. Start off strong and cheerful, and <u>one</u> will be facing the day with a positive outlook. On the other hand, if <u>we</u> wake up in a so-so mood, chances are good that <u>your</u> so-so mood will carry over through the rest of the day and make it so-so. There's no mystery in this: It's simply a matter of common sense. The mood <u>you</u> wake up in sets the tone for the rest of <u>one's</u> day.

Here is the correction using *you. We* or *one* would also be correct, as long as you don't shift from one pronoun to another.

How <u>you</u> wake up in the morning affects how <u>you</u> view the rest of the day. If <u>you</u> start the day off badly, <u>you'll</u> be in a bad mood for the rest of the day. Start off strong and cheerful, and <u>you</u> will be facing the day with a positive outlook. On the other hand, if <u>you</u> wake up in a so-so mood, chances are good that <u>your</u> so-so mood will carry over through the rest of the day and make it so-so. There's no mystery in this: It's simply a matter of common sense. The mood <u>you</u> wake up in sets the tone for the rest of <u>your</u> day.

PRACTICE 1

Correct the shifts in point of view in the following sentences by crossing out and rewriting words when necessary.

1. One should brush their teeth after every meal.

2. They stood in line all day, just to get one's tickets.

3. In spite of my attempt to do the right thing, you could see there was no way to win.

4. A person should study hard if you want to be a success in college.

5. The counselor at the school is a sympathetic person that one can share your troubles with.

6. If one intends to drive for a long time, you should try to get enough sleep the day before.

7. To overcome your bad habits, we should all practice willpower.

8. For someone to succeed in a new job, we must be willing to watch and learn.

9. One's love of ice cream can easily overcome your desire to stay on a diet.

10. I don't play the lottery because you know you can't win.

PRACTICE 2

Complete each of these sentences using a pronoun. Do not shift point of view.

1. When you go out on a blind date _____.

2. If a person exercises, _____.

3. Even though I'm a big baseball fan ———————————.

4. If you pay attention to the big things ———————————.

5. I made several phone calls, but ———————————.

6. You should floss twice a day if ———————————.

7. A person who likes poetry ———————————.

8. If someone wants to save money grocery shopping ——————.

9. A person who likes Chinese food should ——————————.

10. Should you feel restless ———————————.

PRACTICE 3

Rewrite the following sentences to correct the shifts in point of view.

1. If you like to read, one should try the local library.

   ———————————————————————————

   ———————————————————————————

2. One should not talk too much if you don't know the subject well.

   ———————————————————————————

   ———————————————————————————

3. When you go on a trip, one should always have your insurance paid up.

   ———————————————————————————

   ———————————————————————————

4. A person can get good bargains if you shop at outlet stores.

   ———————————————————————————

   ———————————————————————————

5. Someone can make new friends in a city if you join a health club.

   ———————————————————————————

   ———————————————————————————

6. One only has to listen to know that you can't take anything they say at face value.

   ———————————————————————————

   ———————————————————————————

7. Broccoli will help one's digestion, but carrots will help your night vision.

   ———————————————————————————

   ———————————————————————————

8. As you walk into the room, one can hear the people babbling away.

_____

_____

9. When I bought my blender, you never knew that it would come in so handy.

_____

_____

10. One must try hard at everything one does, or you'll never know if you could succeed.

_____

_____

USAGE MONITOR

hisself, theirself, theirselves, themself

Just banish all four of these words from your vocabulary. They are incorrect uses of *himself* or *themselves*.

Not acceptable:	He always likes to wash his car *hisself.*
Acceptable:	He always likes to wash his car *himself.*
Not acceptable:	They can just blame the accident on *theirself* (or *theirselves* or *themself*).
Acceptable:	They can just blame the accident on *themselves.*

Error 8 Review

Rewrite the following paragraph to correct the shifts in point of view.

As part of freshmen orientation week, some colleges organize a hike in the mountains or even an overnight camping trip. Now, to me, that sounds like a good idea. Imagine how we could bond while you're fighting off mosquitoes, building a fire, or sharing our dried food inside your tents. Starting one's freshman week with a lecture, an English-placement test, and an explanation of the campus rules we're supposed to follow is dull by comparison. But a one- or two-day hike by a lake or in the Sierras encourages students to make new friends quickly while you enjoy a few hours of hiking, cycling, trail exploring, or even canoeing. Then you could gather around a campfire at night while the freshmen ask questions of the older students, who can reassure us that college is fun as well as hard work. I think such an orientation would give me confidence as we face college life.

_____

_____

_____

_____

_____

_____

_____

_____

 To check your progress in meeting this chapter's objectives, log in to **www.mywritinglab.com,** go to the **Study Plan** tab, click on **The 20 Most Common Sentence Errors** and choose **Pronoun Reference and Point of View** from the list of subtopics. Read and view the resources in the **Review Materials** section, and then complete the **Recall, Apply,** and **Write** sets in the **Activities** section.

ERROR

9 UNCLEAR OR MISSING REFERENT

If writing were baseball, the pronoun would be a relief pitcher whose job is temporarily to relieve nouns, who are the starters. In both speech and writing, the **pronoun** is a word used in place of a noun, while the **referent** of a pronoun is the noun it replaces.

Consider this sentence:

> Elaine works, but <u>she</u> is getting her degree at night.

The pronoun is *she;* its referent—the word it refers to—is *Elaine.*

Most of the time, the referent of a pronoun is perfectly clear from the context of the sentence. However, sometimes it isn't. Sometimes a referent is either unclear or altogether missing.

Learning Objective

• Identify referents, their relationships with pronouns, and whether they are clear, unclear, or missing

Unclear Referents

Here is an example of an unclear referent:

> Peggy told Denise that she had made a grave error.

In the above sentence, the referent of the pronoun is unclear. We do not know whether Peggy or Denise made the grave error. Here is the same sentence rewritten to avoid the unclear referent:

> Peggy told Denise, "You have made a grave error."

> or

> Peggy told Denise that Denise had made a grave error.

Sometimes the unclear referent is not a person but an action, feeling, or episode.

Unclear: The service was slow, and the food was cold when it arrived, which really upset Herbert.

Was Herbert upset because the service was slow, because the food was cold, or both?

Clear: Not only was the service slow, but the food was cold, both of which upset Herbert.

123

Another example follows:

> **Unclear:**   The population of the United States is aging, which means that in the future, young people will have much more contact with older people. Many people think this is a good thing.

What does *this* refer to? We do not know. It could refer to the fact that the U.S. population is aging, that young and old will interact more in the future, or both.

> **Clear:**   The population of the United States is aging, which means that in the future, young people will have much more contact with older people. Many people think such increased contact will benefit both young and old.

Note that to get around an unclear referent, you may sometimes need to rewrite one sentence as two.

PRACTICE 1

Rewrite the following sentences so that the pronouns refer clearly to only one referent.

1. Marty decided to move to Costa Rica and study medicine, which his parents couldn't understand.

   _____

   _____

2. She scraped the handrails and the stairs and painted them.

   _____

   _____

3. It was hot, the line was long, and the clerk was slow, which really tried Jack's patience.

   _____

   _____

4. My father said to my brother that he was a good father but a bad husband.

   _____

   _____

5. Betty was a good friend of Mary's until she moved to New York.

   _____

   _____

6. Alexa held a lipstick in one hand and blush powder in the other, putting it on as we laughed about the new styles.

_____

_____

7. Ben told Richard he had been a loyal friend.

_____

_____

8. Stanley and Merle's room was a chaotic mess because he had left everything on the floor or on the bed.

_____

_____

9. There are more laws in place to protect the environment than there used to be, but we still have a long way to go. This surprises many people.

_____

_____

10. Mom and Aunt Lottie went shopping even though she had a bad cold.

_____

_____

Missing Referents

In both speech and writing, we often use pronouns with missing referents. This is especially true of the pronouns *they* and *it*. Here is an example:

> Although my grandfather and my father were farmers, I have no interest in it.

What is *it*? We have a fuzzy idea that by *it*, the writer means "farming," but the word *farming* does not appear in the sentence.

Usually the best way to rewrite such a sentence is to omit the pronoun and provide the missing noun.

> Although my grandfather and my father were farmers, I have no interest in farming.

Here are some more examples:

Missing: Between games, they announced the score.

Who is this mysterious *they* in the sentence?

Clear:	Between games, the announcer called out the score.
Missing:	It says to yield to the driver approaching from your right.
Clear:	The sign says to yield to the driver approaching from your right.

Now we know the identity of the unnamed *It*.

The requirement that every pronoun have a specific and clear referent is not strict. In everyday talk, for example, we do not observe such exactness in pronoun use, because we can always ask, "What?" and get an answer. In writing, however, there's no second chance. Every pronoun must therefore have a specific referent.

PRACTICE 2

Rewrite the following sentences to clarify the pronoun referent.

1. It says the shirt comes in plum, mango, and lime green.

_____

_____

2. My boyfriend is a great cook, but I have no interest in it.

_____

_____

3. They did not allow us to touch the Indian weavings.

_____

_____

4. I deposited the money in my bank, but they haven't posted the correct balance.

_____

_____

5. We were in the middle of registering when they informed us that the class was closed.

_____

_____

6. They refused to give me a refund even after I wrote a firm letter.

_____

_____

7. If you don't have a ticket, they won't let you in.

_____

_____

8. See—it says this is a dead-end street.

_____

_____

9. They say one should not beg a lover to stay faithful.

_____

_____

10. It has an alarm that goes off when you open the door from the outside.

_____

_____

PRACTICE 3

Rewrite the following sentences to correct the pronoun errors.

1. Maggie treated Jeanne and her mother to dinner.

_____

_____

2. When Vladimir lent money to Gorsky, he did not know he would go bankrupt.

_____

_____

3. It says the police caught the burglar.

_____

_____

4. Fred insisted to Woody that his wife was not to blame.

_____

_____

5. There is a big difference between the politicians of the past and those of today. They lack nobility.

_____

_____

6. We found a pressed rose in the book that my grandmother had given my grandfather.

_____

_____

7. They allow you to make three separate payments.

_____

_____

8. The nurse told Emma that she liked her name.

_____

_____

9. They say that gelatin is good for your nails.

_____

_____

10. If your Persian cat will not eat raw fish, boil it.

_____

_____

USAGE MONITOR

You and *they* are the two worst pronoun offenders that encourage writers to be hazy. Study the following examples:

> Everyone knows that *you* shouldn't drink raw milk. (Who exactly is *you*?)
>
> **Better:** Everyone knows that *children* shouldn't drink raw milk.
>
> In Somalia, *they* treat women poorly. (Who exactly is *they*?)
>
> **Better:** In Somalia, *men* treat women poorly.

The rule is simple: Avoid using the pronoun *you* or *they* when it doesn't stand for a precise group.

Error 9 Review

Rewrite the following paragraph to eliminate all the pronoun referent problems.

> My friend, Lucy, loves her cat, Fluffy, so much that she purrs constantly. When she takes her to the veterinarian, she orders a limousine so she can hold her and pet her, and so she can feed her little pieces of shrimp, which I think is a bit extreme. Once, Lucy told a neighboring woman that she was noble because she loved cats. They say that women who love cats make good mothers. It wouldn't surprise me. Now, I admire cats because they have such independent spirits, but I do not intend to get one. The other day I saw Lucy's cat holding a real mouse in one paw and a toy mouse in the other, eating it as she frisked and pranced. As long as cat owners outnumber cats, they will not be a problem.

_____

_____

_____

_____

_____

_____

_____

To check your progress in meeting this chapter's objectives, log in to **www.mywritinglab.com,** go to the **Study Plan** tab, click on **The 20 Most Common Sentence Errors** and choose **Pronoun Reference and Point of View** from the list of subtopics. Read and view the resources in the **Review Materials** section, and then complete the **Recall, Apply,** and **Write** sets in the **Activities** section.

10 LACK OF PRONOUN AGREEMENT AND SEXISM

Lack of Pronoun Agreement

A pronoun and its referent (the noun it replaces) must agree in number. Singular nouns require singular pronouns. Plural nouns require plural pronouns. Here are some examples:

The bride put on her veil.

The attendants picked up their flowers.

In the first sentence, the singular noun *bride* requires the singular pronoun *her*. In the second sentence, the plural noun *attendants* requires the plural pronoun *their*.

Although pronoun agreement is often not a problem, it can be a problem when we try to find a pronoun to replace an indefinite pronoun.

An **indefinite pronoun** is a pronoun that refers to no one in particular. Here is a list of common indefinite pronouns (they are always singular):

INDEFINITE PRONOUNS		
one	nobody	each
anyone	anybody	either
everyone	everybody	neither
someone	somebody	

Study these sentences:

Incorrect:	Each of the men carry a bottle of water.
Correct:	Each of the men carries a bottle of water.
	(*Each* requires a singular pronoun. Remember, cross out the prepositional phrase if you are confused about who the subject is.)
Incorrect:	Either Harriet or Nancy will give me their paycheck.
Correct:	Either Harriet or Nancy will give me her paycheck.
	(*Either* requires a singular pronoun.)

In both speech and writing, to avoid being sexist, we often use the plural *their* to refer to many indefinite pronouns that are singular. For example, we say the following, and it sounds perfectly right to our ear:

Someone put their keys on the table.

Technically speaking, this use is wrong. *Their* is plural; *Someone* is singular. On the other hand, the singular pronoun *his* is sexist:

Someone put his keys on the table.

It is sexist because *Someone* could be a female, a possibility the pronoun *his* ignores.

The best way to correct an agreement problem is to rewrite the sentence. You can change the wrong pronoun either to singular or plural. Here is an example:

Incorrect: Everyone who donates $50 will get their name on a plaque.
Correct: If you donate $50, you will get your name on a plaque.
Correct: People who donate $50 will get their names on a plaque.

Here is another example:

Incorrect: Did everyone have their coffee?
Correct: Did every diner have his or her coffee?
Correct: Did all the diners have their coffee?

PRACTICE 1

Correct the agreement errors in the following sentences both ways that you've learned—by changing the pronoun to the singular and to the plural.

1. Is everybody bringing their date to the party?

Singular: _____

_____

Plural: _____

_____

2. Everyone should help themselves to dessert.

Singular: _____

_____

Plural: _____

_____

3. Nobody knows for certain what their future holds.

Singular: _____

_____

Plural: _____

_____

4. If anyone needs help, they should ask me.

Singular: _____

_____

Plural: _____

_____

5. Would everyone who saw the accident give me their names?

Singular: _____

_____

Plural: _____

_____

6. If everyone did what they were told, the world would be a better place.

Singular: _____

_____

Plural: _____

_____

7. If someone tries hard, they will be sure to succeed.

Singular: _____

_____

Plural: _____

_____

8. If someone has a problem with a co-worker, they should try to work it out privately.

Singular: _____

_____

Plural: _____

_____

9. Will everyone please tell us their names?

Singular: _____

_____

Plural: _____

_____

10. Neither Dennis nor Derrick sent in their money.

Singular: _____

_____

Plural: _____

_____

Sexism in Writing

You have just learned how to avoid the sexist use of indefinite pronouns. Sexism in writing is even worse when a singular pronoun automatically assigns the male sex to professionals:

>   Every police officer should wear his badge at all times.

The use of *his* in the above sentence suggests that every police officer is a man, which is both sexist and untrue. On the other hand, using *his or her* is correct but clumsy. Another solution is to make the whole sentence plural, using the neutral pronoun *their*. The possible nonsexist choices follow.

Incorrect: Every police officer should wear his badge at all times.

Correct: Every police officer should wear his or her badge at all times.

Correct: Police officers should wear their badges at all times.

Their includes both men and women, and it is not as clumsy as *his or her.*

On the other hand, sometimes we are quick to assume that some professions are dominated by women. For example, we might refer to a nurse, a secretary, or a grade school teacher as *she*. This is also sexist because both men and women can be nurses, secretaries, and grade school teachers. Here is an example of this type of sexism in writing:

Incorrect: An elementary school teacher should be a good role model for her students.

Correct: An elementary school teacher should be a good role model for his or her students.

Correct: Elementary school teachers should be good role models for their students.

If you are facing the pronoun agreement problem in which you simply cannot rewrite the pronoun in the plural, then use *his or her.* If the choice is between being sexist or being clumsy, we think it is better to be clumsy.

PRACTICE 2

Rewrite the following sentences to correct the sexist bias.

1. When a plumber is finished working, he shouldn't leave a mess for the customer.

   _____

   _____

2. A hairstylist should always keep her station clean.

   _____

   _____

3. A good secretary keeps her boss organized.

   _____

   _____

4. A flight attendant should be sure her uniform is clean and pressed.

_____

_____

5. You could call a lawyer and find out what he thinks.

_____

_____

6. A social worker visits her clients regularly to check their progress.

_____

_____

7. A criminal who breaks the law repeatedly should serve his full jail term.

_____

_____

8. A reporter must check his facts carefully.

_____

_____

9. An archaeologist in the field should take care of his digging tools.

_____

_____

10. If your doctor doesn't give you an itemized bill, ask him for one.

_____

_____

USAGE MONITOR

Sexist nouns

Some nouns in the English language are traditionally sexist. Here are some of the worst offenders and their alternatives:

Sexist	Alternative
man	person
mankind	people, human beings
chairman	chair, chairperson
mailman	mail carrier
policeman	police officer
fireman	firefighter
congressman	member of Congress

PRACTICE 3

Rewrite the following sentences to correct the agreement errors and sexism.

1. Everyone should call their mother at least once a month.

_____

_____

2. Neither Nicole nor Sally turned in their homework.

_____

_____

3. A professor should be available to help her students.

_____

_____

4. Either my dog or my cat will get their shots today.

_____

_____

5. Everyone knows that they should not walk on the grass when it is wet.

_____

_____

6. A good boss plans her day efficiently.

_____

_____

7. Nobody in their right mind would do such a thing.

_____

_____

8. An architect needs his blueprints to present his ideas.

_____

_____

9. Everybody wanted their refunds by mail.

_____

_____

10. An obstetrician should be considerate of his pregnant patients.

_____

_____

Error 10 Review

Rewrite the following paragraph to correct all pronoun agreement and sexism errors.

One problem I have with our neighborhood grocery store is that they hide flawed fruits and vegetables behind fruits and vegetables that are perfect. For instance, the other day, I was in the mood for a juicy nectarine. So, I drove to Tim's Market. In the back of the store, I spied a bin heaped with gorgeous yellowish-red nectarines. With eager anticipation I gently palpated the top row of the heap to confirm that each of the globes were perfectly ripe—just ready to be eaten in heavenly, juicy bites. Everyone around me were also admiring the fabulous display. No one indicated that they suspected anything was wrong with the fruit. But when I started lifting off the top nectarines, I found that the nectarines in the layers underneath were bruised, small, or hard. Each of these nectarines were of inferior quality. None were like the large, attractive, ripe fruit adorning the top layer. It seems to me that when someone owns a grocery store, they should not pretend that all the fruit they sell is top quality. Damaged fruit and vegetables should be placed in a special bin to be sold at a lower price. Every grocery owner should respect his clients enough to be truly honest in his marketing strategies.

_____

_____

_____

_____

_____

_____

_____

_____

_____

_____

_____

To check your progress in meeting this chapter's objectives, log in to **www.mywritinglab.com,** go to the **Study Plan** tab, click on **The 20 Most Common Sentence Errors** and choose **Pronoun-Antecedent Agreement and Pronoun Case** from the list of subtopics. Read and view the resources in the **Review Materials** section, and then complete the **Recall, Apply,** and **Write** sets in the **Activities** section.

TROUBLE WITH USING ADVERBS AND ADJECTIVES IN COMPARISONS AND SUPERLATIVES

Adjectives and adverbs are **modifiers,** words that describe and explain. **Adjectives** describe a noun or a pronoun by narrowing it down to a specific type, such as in the following cases:

I envy that thin girl.	**(Which girl? the *thin* one)**
She feels lonely.	**(How does she feel? *lonely*)**
The apples look ripe.	**(How do the apples look? *ripe*)**

Learning Objective

• Understand the difference between adverbs and adjectives for comparisons and superlatives

Adverbs describe verbs, adjectives, and other adverbs in the following ways:

• They tell *how.*

• They tell *when.*

• They tell *where.*

• They tell *to what extent.*

Many adverbs end in *-ly:* for example, *neatly, roughly, slowly, totally, considerably, really, terribly, scarcely.* But others—such as *soon, fast, hard, well, yesterday, tomorrow, nearby,* and *very*—do not. Here are some examples of how adverbs (underlined) are used in a sentence.

She ran <u>very</u> quickly.	(***Very*** tells how she ran—describes the adverb *quickly.*)
We're leaving <u>soon</u>.	(***Soon*** tells when we're leaving—describes the verb *leaving.*)
He stood <u>here</u>.	(***Here*** tells where he stood—describes the verb *stood.*)
They are <u>terribly</u> late.	(***Terribly*** tells to what extent they are late—describes the adverb *late.*)
The star of the movie was <u>exceptionally</u> beautiful.	(***Exceptionally*** describes the adjective *beautiful.*)

USAGE MONITOR

A few adjectives, like *friendly,* end in *-ly* and might cause you to mistake them for adverbs. For instance, don't be fooled into writing, "She spoke *friendly.*" (*Friendly* is not an adverb.) Instead, write, "She spoke in a *friendly* manner." Moreover, some words, like *real,* are often misused. While it is correct to say, "This is a *real* diamond," it is not correct to say, "We ate a *real* good meal last night." In the first case, you need an adjective to modify the noun *diamond.* In the second case, you need an adverb to modify the adjective *good.* Here's the correct way: "We ate a *really* good meal last night."

PRACTICE 1

In the blank, write *adv* if the underlined word is an adverb or *adj* if it is an adjective.

1. ____   Jim drives <u>fast</u> to work.

2. ____   The sharks swam in the <u>cold</u> ocean.

3. ____   Beverly tries to be a <u>thoughtful</u> friend.

4. ____   She jumped <u>immediately</u>.

5. ____   The wind felt <u>chilly</u>.

6. ____   It was an <u>extremely</u> difficult test.

7. ____   She called <u>desperately</u> for help.

8. ____   They disappeared into the <u>deep</u> forest.

9. ____   I slept through the <u>boring</u> movie.

10. ____   It was a <u>truly</u> magnificent morning.

Comparisons

Adjectives and adverbs are often used to make comparisons between two things. The rules for making comparisons are straightforward:

- For an adjective or adverb of one syllable, add *-er:*

  The bread is warm.   **(One-syllable adjective)**
  The rolls are warmer.

  He swallowed hard.   **(One-syllable adverb)**
  She swallowed harder.

- For an adjective or adverb of more than one syllable, add *more:*

  The book was shocking.   **(Adjective of more than one**
  The movie was more shocking.   **syllable)**

  Our camp rebelled openly.   **(Adverb of more than one**
  Their camp rebelled even more openly.   **syllable)**

- For an adjective or adverb that ends in *-y*, drop the *-y* and add *-ier* in the comparative:

She's lucky at love.

She's luckier at cards.

Jerry is funny.

Mary is funnier.

PRACTICE 2

Write the comparative form of each word listed below.

Example: long   <u>longer</u>

          beautiful   <u>more beautiful</u>

1. messy _____

2. blunt _____

3. furious _____

4. desirable _____

5. cold _____

6. goofy _____

7. mean _____

8. clumsy _____

9. intelligent _____

10. happy _____

Double comparisons

A common mistake often heard in everyday speech is the **double comparison,** which uses both *-er* and *more*.

Incorrect:	Phoenix is more hotter than San Francisco.
Correct:	Phoenix is hotter than San Francisco.
Incorrect:	Bunny is more quieter than Lisa.
Correct:	Bunny is quieter than Lisa.

PRACTICE 3

Rewrite the following sentences to correct the comparisons.

1. Wayne has the more calmer attitude.

_____

_____

2. The sooner you leave, the more faster you will get there.

_____

_____

3. Her hairdo is attractiver than Joyce's.

_____

_____

4. This story is more sadder than I expected.

_____

_____

5. She was at peace and more serener than before.

_____

_____

6. Squirrels are much more quicker than rabbits.

_____

_____

7. Where freedom is concerned, Americans are more luckier than most other citizens.

_____

_____

8. When can we afford a more better car?

_____

_____

9. He traveled oftener than he had told me.

_____

_____

10. The ocean was dangerouser than it looked.

_____

_____

Superlatives

The comparative form of adjectives and adverbs is used to express a difference between two things.

> The first bell is loud.
> The second bell is louder.   **(Comparative)**

To express differences among three or more things, you must use the superlative form of an adjective or adverb.

The first bell is loud.

The second bell is louder.   **(Comparative)**

The third bell is loudest.   **(Superlative)**

The salmon is fresh.

The swordfish is fresher.   **(Comparative)**

The trout is freshest of all.   **(Superlative)**

The rules for changing adjectives and adverbs into the superlative form are simple:

- For an adverb or adjective of one syllable, add *-est:*

dark	darker	darkest
light	lighter	lightest
short	shorter	shortest

He was the shortest of all the basketball players.

Notice that some adjectives or adverbs double the final consonant: *gladder / gladdest, sadder / saddest, dimmer / dimmest, bigger / biggest.*

- For an adjective that ends in *-y,* drop the *-y* and add *-iest:*

funny	funnier	funniest
fancy	fancier	fanciest
petty	pettier	pettiest

Marty was the craziest of them all.

For an adjective or adverb of two or more syllables, add the word *most:*

wonderful	more wonderful	most wonderful
fortunate	more fortunate	most fortunate
interesting	more interesting	most interesting

Loons make the most dreadful sound at night.

PRACTICE 4

In the blanks provided, write the correct superlative forms of the words below.

1. _____ merciful

2. _____ skinny

3. _____ sweet

4. _____ carefully

5. _____ pushy

6. _____ smoothly

7. _____ thoughtful

8. _____ hideous

9. _____ unusual

10. _____ thick

Problems with superlatives

When you use superlatives, watch out for these common errors of everyday speech:

- Use the superlative only when you are speaking of *more than two things:*

Incorrect:	She is the most qualified of the two applicants.
Correct:	She is the more qualified of the two applicants.
Incorrect:	This is the funniest of the two scenes.
Correct:	This is the funnier of the two scenes.

- Do not use both an *-est* or an *-iest* ending and *most:*

Incorrect:	That is the most kindest gesture imaginable.
Correct:	That is the kindest gesture imaginable.
Incorrect:	She has the most sunniest disposition.
Correct:	She has the sunniest disposition.

PRACTICE 5

Rewrite the following sentences to correct the errors in forming the superlative.

1. Isn't this place the most wonderfulest you could ever imagine?

_____

_____

2. Both models on the cover are the beautifulest.

_____

_____

3. This is the most hardest math assignment I have ever been given.

_____

_____

4. Older people can give you the most wisest counsel of all.

_____

_____

5. Of the three, she is the most youngest.

_____

_____

6. Have the judges given out the gold medal to the most worthiest of the three athletes?

_____

_____

7. Many people find Irish storytellers the interestingest of all English-language writers.

_____

_____

8. Miami's the most hottest city imaginable in the summer.

_____

_____

9. Our choir has the most talentedest singers.

_____

_____

10. The biggest cities are bound to harbor the corruptest criminals.

_____

_____

PRACTICE 6

For the following sentences, first decide whether a comparative or a superlative form is needed. Then write the correct form.

Example: It was the (beautiful) <u>most beautiful</u> rainbow I'd ever seen.

1. She is the (fanatic) _____ person I have ever met.

2. Of the two dogs, the boxer was the (friendly) _____.

3. The Arco Building seemed to be the (high) _____ building I had ever seen.

4. Of all the office managers, she was the (efficient) _____.

5. A ripe peach is (sweet) _____ than a ripe plum.

6. Of the two candles, the red one was the (pretty) _____.

7. Uncle George was the (ambitious) _____ member of my dad's family.

8. Consider the three routes, and then take the (fast) _____.

9. We were asked to relate the (embarrassing) _____ moment of our childhood.

10. The bridge is (slippery) _____ than the road when it rains.

Error 11 Review

Rewrite the passage that follows to correct all incorrect comparatives or superlatives.

When there is a choice at the grocery store, I always ask for a plastic bag rather than a paper one. First of all, plastic bags are usefuller than paper ones because you can use them as small garbage can liners or as handy travel bags. Second of all, plastic bags are more stronger than paper ones. If a paper bag gets the least bit damp, it tears, and all of its contents spill out—sometimes causing the embarrassingest situation imaginable. People rush to your aid thinking, "This shopper is more clumsy than a clown." Besides, plastic bags preserve trees because to make paper bags, you have to cut down trees. I show off that I am more environmentally consciouser than shoppers with paper bags when I exit from the grocery store. It's best to bring your own bag, of course, but if you forget it, using plastic instead of paper grocery bags is one of the most easiest ways to be environmentally conscious.

_____

_____

_____

_____

_____

_____

_____

_____

 To check your progress in meeting this chapter's objectives, log in to **www.mywritinglab.com,** go to the **Study Plan** tab, click on **The 20 Most Common Sentence Errors** and choose **Adverbs and Adjectives** from the list of subtopics. Read and view the resources in the **Review Materials** section, and then complete the **Recall, Apply,** and **Write** sets in the **Activities** section.

ERROR

12

DANGLING OR MISPLACED MODIFIERS

Bizzaro (new) © 2007 Dan Piraro.
King Features Syndicate

Having gone up and refused to come down, I hereby find you in violation of the law.

PHYSICS COURT

Learning Objective

- Identify modifiers and determine whether they are dangling or misplaced

A **modifier** is a word or phrase that describes something. Modifiers can be adjectives, adverbs, or words or phrases that function as adjectives or adverbs. What a modifier describes in a sentence depends not only on what it says, but also on where it is placed in the sentence.

> Snapping violently, the tourists ran from the alligator.

Here, *Snapping violently* is a modifier. Because of its place in the sentence, however, it modifies *tourists* rather than *alligator*. Such a modifier is said to dangle.

Dangling Modifiers

A **dangling modifier** is a word or phrase at the beginning of a sentence that mistakenly modifies the word that immediately follows it—"mistakenly" because it was intended to modify a different word. When a modifier begins a sentence, *the word it modifies must come immediately after it*. Otherwise, the modifier will be unconnected to the word the writer meant it to modify. In short, it will dangle. Here are some examples:

Dangling: Dipping below the horizon, I watched as the sun set.

Dangling: Confused and upset, the crowded store caused the little girl to lose her mother.

Dangling: Screeching, we looked for our binoculars as the owl flew by.

147

To correct these sentences, place the word being modified immediately after the modifier and rewrite as necessary.

Correct:	Dipping below the horizon, the sun set as I watched.
Correct:	Confused and upset, the little girl lost her mother in the crowded store.
Correct:	Screeching, the owl flew by as we looked for our binoculars.

Sometimes correcting a dangling modifier results in the passive voice. In this case, restructure the sentence completely. Here is an example:

Dangling:	Hiding under a rock, I found a little lizard.
Correct but passive voice:	Hiding under a rock, a little lizard was found by me.
Correct and active voice:	I found a little lizard hiding under a rock.

PRACTICE 1

Rewrite these sentences to correct the dangling modifiers.

1. Fluttering wildly, I caught the butterfly in my net.

   _____

   _____

2. Newly polished, the guests marveled at the gleaming silverware.

   _____

   _____

3. Hurrying through the grocery store, my shopping bag seemed especially heavy.

   _____

   _____

4. Old and broken, she left the couch behind when she moved.

   _____

   _____

5. Drooping pitifully, I watered the plant.

   _____

   _____

6. Drenched from the recent rain, he still watered the lawn.

   _____

   _____

7. Weeping on stage, the audience was enthralled by the actor.

   _____

   _____

8. Pounded by waves and sinking at the stern, I watched the ship go down.

_____

_____

9. As an athlete, weight training is very important.

_____

_____

10. Wearing my new glasses, the stars in the sky looked beautiful.

_____

_____

Misplaced Modifiers

A modifier tends to modify the nearest noun. For example, notice how the meaning of the following sentence changes as we move the modifier *only:*

She went into the pool wearing her only bikini.	**(She owned only one bikini. *Only* is modifying *bikini*.)**
She went into the pool wearing only her bikini.	**(She wore nothing but a bikini. *Only* is modifying *wearing*.)**

A **misplaced modifier** is too far from the word it is meant to modify, and as a result, it doesn't convey the correct meaning *or* it gives the sentence an unintended, funny meaning. Here are some examples of misplaced modifiers with unintentional meanings:

Misplaced:	The fisherman caught a bass with a chuckle.
Misplaced:	I climbed a tree with new shoes on.
Misplaced:	She bicycled to Burlington to visit her grandmother wearing a bike helmet.

Because of misplaced modifiers, we have *a bass with a chuckle, a tree with new shoes,* and a *grandmother wearing a bike helmet.* A misplaced modifier is corrected by rewriting the sentence. You must reword the modifier or move it closer to the word it modifies. Here are possible corrections:

With a chuckle, the fisherman caught a bass.

With new shoes on, I climbed the tree.

Wearing a bike helmet, she bicycled to Burlington to visit her grandmother.

USAGE MONITOR

Misplaced modifiers are perfect fodder for comedians seeking to amuse an audience, as in this famous statement attributed to Groucho Marx: "The other day I shot an elephant in my pajamas. How he got in my pajamas, I'll never know."

To avoid confusing your reader with misplaced modifiers, always place a modifier immediately in front of the word it is meant to modify. This is especially true of one-word modifiers such as *almost, even, hardly, nearly, only,* and *often.* Because these words limit what follows, their placement in a sentence is important. Remember the bikini example at the beginning of this section. Another example follows.

He just baked a cake.	**(He did it a moment ago.)**
He baked just a cake.	**(He didn't bake bread.)**

PRACTICE 2

First underline the misplaced modifier in each sentence below. Then rewrite the sentence so that the modifier is correctly placed.

Example: I put money in the bank <u>with a smile. With a smile, I put money in the bank.</u>

1. Jonathan gave his dog a bone with a pat on the head.

_____

_____

2. At the ceremony, he retired with honors in his uniform.

_____

_____

3. The pool table seemed tilted to the customers.

_____

_____

4. We saw huge fir trees skiing down the slope on both sides.

_____

_____

5. Josephine barbecued ribs for 20 people on the grill.

_____

_____

6. The jogger ran past the dog wearing a funny hat.

_____

_____

7. Spaghetti is most delicious when it is eaten on a patio with meatballs.

_____

_____

8. She almost handed out candy to the trick-or-treaters for two hours.

_____

_____

9. We saw the ocean waves sitting on a deck.

_____

_____

10. The young lovers admired the moon going on a stroll.

_____

_____

Error 12 Review

Underline the dangling and misplaced modifiers in the following paragraph. Then rewrite the sentences correctly on the lines below. You should find six errors.

My favorite place during the summer is the beach. Relaxing on the sand, the waves roll in peacefully. Seagulls look for crabs overhead. When I'm on the beach, my mind is full of nothing but relaxation and pleasant dreams playing in the sand. Buzzing noisily, I ignore the hordes of flies. Occasionally, I wade into the surf and enjoy watching the waves up close with my shoes on. Thinking of neither work nor school, the beach is pure pleasure. In fact, when I'm on the beach, I think of nothing at all, except how lovely it is to be there.

_____

_____

_____

_____

_____

_____

To check your progress in meeting this chapter's objectives, log in to **www.mywritinglab.com,** go to the **Study Plan** tab, click on **The 20 Most Common Sentence Errors** and choose **Dangling or Misplaced Modifiers** and **Modifiers** from the list of subtopics. Read and view the resources in the **Review Materials** section, and then complete the **Recall, Apply,** and **Write** sets in the **Activities** section.

13 OMITTED COMMAS, PART I

Punctuation marks are the road signs of writing that tell the reader when to slow down, when to speed up, and when to stop. In spoken sentences, punctuation is heard as pauses, upbeats, and downbeats.

Learning Objective

• Understand the importance of punctuation for reading pace, how commas can change sentence meaning, and how commas combine dependent clauses

The Comma (,)

You hear the comma as a half-pause. Sometimes the comma just makes listening or reading easier, but sometimes it is crucial to meaning. Here is an example:

> Still, water was important to many primitive tribes.

> Still water was important to many primitive tribes.

The meanings of these two sentences depend on where the comma is placed. In the first sentence, *Still* means "nonetheless" or "nevertheless." In the second sentence, *Still* serves as an adjective describing *water*.

In this section we will cover two hard-and-fast rules of comma usage.

Commas with coordinating conjunctions

Place a comma in front of coordinating conjunctions (*and, but, or, for, nor, so, yet*) that link independent clauses (see Unit 4 "Building Sentences").

> He dated Mabel, but he did not fall in love with her.

> I am obsessed with neatness, and my girlfriend is, too.

> He wrote me three letters, so I finally answered him.

Do not use a comma before *and* if it is not followed by an independent clause.

Incorrect:	He read a magazine, and watched TV.
Correct:	He read a magazine and watched TV.

USAGE MONITOR

Here's an easy rule to keep in mind: If the second clause does not begin with a noun or pronoun, don't use a comma.

Incorrect:	Max knows how to use his new rip stick, and loves to show off on it. (No comma needed)
Correct:	Max knows how to use his new rip stick, and he loves to show off on it. (Comma needed)

or

Mom likes Mrs. Mueter, and Mrs. Mueter likes Mom. (Comma needed)

PRACTICE 1

Finish the following sentences by adding another independent clause and a coordinating conjunction. Remember to use a comma.

Example: The clouds were beautiful.

<u>The clouds were beautiful, but they brought heavy rain.</u>

1. The earth is mother to us all _____

2. I love movies _____

3. On July 4 we always have a picnic _____

4. Make a fresh pot of coffee _____

5. Love is what makes the world happy _____

6. Fred plays the violin in private _____

7. We're good friends _____

8. Many people are utterly sincere _____

9. The dew was on the rose _____

10. Jane should stop feeling sorry for herself _____

Commas with introductory words, phrases, and clauses

Use a comma after introductory words, phrases, and clauses.

Words:	Therefore, we beg you to be patient.
	Well, I am not the least bit surprised.
	Derrick, I'll take full responsibility.
Phrases:	Seen from the top of the hill, the church was small.
	Having expressed my view, I withdrew from the argument.
	By the way, you owe me $10.

Use a comma after a dependent clause only when it comes at the beginning, not at the end, of a sentence:

If at first you don't succeed, try again.

but

Try again if at first you don't succeed.

When I get a raise, I'm getting a new suit.

but

I'm getting a new suit when I get a raise.

PRACTICE 2

Insert commas where needed. Mark *C* for correct if no comma is needed.

1. ____   No they cannot enter without paying a fee.

2. ____   If he is a great man then many men are great.

3. ____   Although he had a headache Clarence continued to run.

4. ____   Take a left on Elm Street and then a right at the first light.

5. ____   She made a budget but she is not sticking to it.

6. ____   Nevertheless high heels are bad for your posture.

7. ____   I have two job interviews tomorrow and one on Monday.

8. ____   When we live by the sword we perish by the sword.

9. ____   First of all finding happiness should not be your primary goal.

10. ____   He hates to give speeches but he always agrees to do so when it's for a good cause.

PRACTICE 3

Insert commas where needed. In the spaces provided, state the rule that makes the comma necessary.

Example: Ted, your dad is looking for you.

RULE: <u>A comma follows an introductory word.</u>

1. Because I am a woman I believe that mothers influence sons.

    Rule: _____

    _____

2. Serena please pass the salt and pepper.

    Rule: _____

    _____

3. She accepted the gold trophy and he accepted the blue ribbon.

Rule: _____

_____

4. Knowing the consequences of leaving we stayed at home.

Rule: _____

_____

5. Additionally he stole her wallet.

Rule: _____

_____

6. The lightning bolt flashed across the sky and rain poured from the heavens.

Rule: _____

_____

7. From where I sit I have observed some fascinating people.

Rule: _____

_____

8. Although he hates routine he orders his coffee at 7:00 A.M. every morning.

Rule: _____

_____

9. Are they planning to pick you up or are you driving alone?

Rule: _____

_____

10. If you hate your job your health is bound to be affected.

Rule: _____

_____

Error 13 Review

Correct the passage that follows by placing commas where they belong.

Parents and grandparents who don't learn to use the Internet are behind the times and their situation will only get worse. From a commonsense point of view computer literacy is a modern requirement. If you think about it learning to use computers today is equivalent to learning to drive a car 50 years ago. The library in my hometown sponsors several media literacy classes and our local community college offers special workshops in using the Internet. These classes teach adults basic skills and how to connect with the World Wide Web. They even receive tips on how to supervise their children's use of the Internet. My mother has not yet taken advantage of these classes.

Therefore she knows nothing about the technology her children use every day. However, our neighbor took a computer course and enjoyed it very much. If this neighbor's enthusiasm influences my mother to sign up for the class I'll be thrilled. She might then become technologically literate and part of the 21st century.

To check your progress in meeting this chapter's objectives, log in to **www.mywritinglab.com,** go to the **Study Plan** tab, click on **The 20 Most Common Sentence Errors** and choose **Commas** from the list of subtopics. Read and view the resources in the **Review Materials** section, and then complete the **Recall, Apply,** and **Write** sets in the **Activities** section.

14 OMITTED COMMAS, PART II

I n Error 13, you learned two rules for using commas:

1. Place a comma in front of coordinating conjunctions (*and, but, or, for, nor, so, yet*) that link independent clauses.

2. Use a comma after introductory words, phrases, and clauses.

In this section, you will learn two more hard-and-fast rules for using commas:

1. Use commas to separate items in a series.

2. Place commas around words that interrupt the flow of a sentence.

Learning Objective

- Understand the use of commas in lists and in interrupting sentence flow

Use commas to separate items in a series

We can talk, daydream, play cards, or read.

They swam, played football, and threw the Frisbee.

The soft, furry leaves feel like velvet.

We will research the facts, gather support, and publicize our cause.

Do not, however, use commas unnecessarily with words in a series.

Do not use a comma before "and" if only two items are mentioned

Incorrect:	He reads novels, and poetry.
Correct:	He reads novels and poetry.

Do not use a comma between modifiers unless you can insert the word "and" between them

Incorrect:	She carried beautiful, red roses.
Correct:	She carried beautiful red roses.

You wouldn't say, "She carried beautiful and red roses," so you shouldn't use a comma. You would, however, use a comma between the modifiers of this sentence:

> A fresh, exhilarating breeze blew off the ocean.

You could insert an *and* between the modifiers, and the sentence would still sound right:

> A fresh and exhilarating breeze blew off the ocean.

USAGE MONITOR

and etc. or *and, etc.*

The word *and* used in combination with *etc.* is plain surplus. *Etc.* is an abbreviation for the Latin *et cetera,* meaning "<u>and</u> the rest." We recommend that you avoid using this Latin term and instead use the English "and so forth" or spell out the additional information.

Here's some advice for ESL students:
If you can't hear the incorrectness of the sentence, memorize the rule.

Do not use a comma before the first or after the last item in a series

Incorrect: We went, to sightsee, to shop, to dine out, and to enjoy, ourselves.

Correct: We went to sightsee, to shop, to dine out, and to enjoy ourselves.

Incorrect: She put, her shoes, her handbag, and her suitcase, in the trunk of the car.

Correct: She put her shoes, her handbag, and her suitcase in the trunk of the car.

PRACTICE 1

Insert commas as necessary to separate items in a series.

1. They jumped over rocks trees and bushes.

2. We can do the job with a little luck a little effort and a little perseverance.

3. I love you more than chocolate marshmallows apple pie and fudge brownies.

4. You need paper pencil and your textbook.

5. Bright sparkling water gushed from the beautiful old fountain.

6. They ate pasta bread and peanuts to get ready for the race.

7. I have a dog a cat a bird and a snake.

8. Do you prefer yams bananas or plantains?

9. My mother my father my sister and my brother live with me.

10. I like to watch baseball football tennis and soccer on television.

PRACTICE 2

Strike through the unnecessary commas in the following sentences.

Example: The old lady put down her coat, and hat.

1. She runs, lifts weights, and eats plenty of fresh vegetables, to keep fit.

2. I love my house, and my garden.

3. My neighbors include, a Jamaican, an American, and an Armenian.

4. My ugly, blue car is in the garage.

5. Pack sandwiches, fruit, drinks, and cookies, for the picnic.

6. I love Beethoven, and Chopin.

7. Among my uncle's favorite foods, are ice cream, apples, peaches, and apricots.

8. The brand, new Jeep belongs to my roommate.

9. The card games we like include, canasta, gin, poker, and hearts.

10. The band played blues, and rock and roll.

Place commas around words that interrupt the flow of a sentence

In talking, it is natural to pause before and after words that interrupt the flow of thought. In writing, this pause is signaled by commas. Interruptions include the following:

1. Expression

   You understand, of course, that the position is temporary.

2. Descriptive phrase

   The lighthouse, tall and majestic, stood among the rocks.
   Mr. Golub, our mail carrier, is always very pleasant.

3. Prepositional phrase

   The ice, to which they'd driven an hour to reach.

4. Unessential clauses that begin with *who, whose, which, when, where,* or *that*

   Elaine, who went to Oakland Community College, now lives in Detroit.

A clause containing information that is *not* essential to understanding a sentence is enclosed by commas.

Ms. Jones, who works at Benson's, witnessed the accident.	(Because Ms. Jones is named, the information in the clause is not essential to identify her as the woman who witnessed the accident.)

On the other hand, a clause containing information essential to understanding the sentence is not set off by commas.

The woman who works at Benson's witnessed the accident.

Now the information in the clause is essential to identify who witnessed the accident—*The woman who works at Benson's*—since we don't know her name.

Commas needed:	The poet recited "Daddy," which I'd never heard before.
Commas not needed:	The poet recited a poem that I'd never heard before.

Most of the time, relative clauses with *which* need commas whereas relative clauses with *that* do not.

Commas needed:	The horse Anchovy, which I often ride, is in the stable.
Commas not needed:	The horse that I often ride is in the stable.

PRACTICE 3

Underline the words that interrupt the flow of each sentence, and then place commas around them.

Example: My uncle who now has gray hair is also my best friend.

My uncle, who now has gray hair, is also my best friend.

1. The beloved teacher who had taught for 50 years finally retired.

2. The divorce which no one expected was final last week.

3. He realized of course that he would never make his plane.

4. My mother a champion rug hooker never took lessons in her art.

5. The old cat purring furiously rubbed up against my leg.

6. The police officer who is also our crossing guard always looks out for the small children.

7. Mr. Smith by the way is a champion chess player.

8. Self-confidence a key ingredient in success can be developed.

9. The garden around which we strolled is very well cared for.

10. You are nevertheless mistaken on that point.

PRACTICE 4

Insert the omitted commas in the following sentences. Use all four rules that you have learned in Errors 13 and 14. Then, in the spaces provided, state the rules you used. If no comma is needed, state the rule that makes it unnecessary.

1. I spoke to him repeatedly but he wouldn't listen.

Rule: _____

2. You need a walking stick a backpack and a compass for the hike.

Rule: _____

3. Of course it is your right to decline.

Rule: _____

4. My Uncle Harry who wears a hearing aid was at my graduation.

Rule: _____

5. Peter will you answer the door?

Rule: _____

6. I wore my new blue blazer.

Rule: _____

7. They had however other plans.

Rule: _____

8. She heard my voice and came into the room.

Rule: _____

9. My best friend who is also my accountant went with me.

Rule: _____

10. Because you're so nice I wanted to give you a gift.

Rule: _____

Error 14 Review

Rewrite the following paragraph, adding commas where needed.

Even with a plan it's easy to get derailed. For example when I started college my goal was to become a pediatric nurse. I concentrated on getting good grades so I studied hard working long hours into the night. My science classes required a tremendous amount of reading memorizing and hours of lab work. But in the spring of my sophomore year I enrolled in a drama class as an elective. I was chosen to be in the school musical and I started to hang out with other drama students. They were all one big bad influence. They spent their days and evenings in the auditorium instead of the classroom. Being young and naïve I took to these devil-may-care people faster than you can say, "Ambisol." As a result my career goals crashed burned and went up in smoke. I neglected reading assignments cut class and skipped labs. All I did was hang around with my new theater friends pretending we were headed for Broadway and fame. When my mother noticed my grades slipping she warned me that my new friends were bad for me but of course I didn't listen. Fortunately the school newspaper panned my performance and I came to my senses. I also realized that I was hurting my mother the person I loved most. So I quit drama and started studying. I am now back to my original hopes and dreams bolstered by diligence and determination.

_____

_____

_____

_____

_____

_____

_____

_____

_____

_____

 To check your progress in meeting this chapter's objectives, log in to **www.mywritinglab.com,** go to the **Study Plan** tab, click on **The 20 Most Common Sentence Errors** and choose **Commas** from the list of subtopics. Read and view the resources in the **Review Materials** section, and then complete the **Recall, Apply,** and **Write** sets in the **Activities** section.

15 APOSTROPHE PROBLEMS

Learning Objective

- Examine and explain how apostrophes indicate possession or contraction and how they are used in other special cases

www.CartoonStock.com

"Some people want to abolish apostrophes – but I'm very possessive about them."

The apostrophe (') has two main uses: to show possession and to indicate a contraction.

Using an Apostrophe to Show Possession

The chart below indicates how apostrophes are used to show possession or ownership. For a singular or plural noun not ending in *s*, always add *'s*. If a singular noun already ends in *s*, add only the apostrophe. If a plural noun already ends in *s*, add only the apostrophe.

SINGULAR	PLURAL
dog's tail	dogs' tails
boss's desk	bosses' desks
woman's hat	women's hats
Genevieve Smith's home	the Smiths' home
Dolores' T-shirt	

PRACTICE 1

Make the following nouns possessive. First decide if the noun is singular or plural. Then decide if you need only an apostrophe or *'s.*

1. The Browns barbecue _____

2. The cat dish _____

3. The doctors offices _____

4. The person mood _____

5. The children games _____

6. The car windshield _____

7. Moses Ten Commandments _____

8. The politicians photograph _____

9. The churches towers _____

10. The barnyard smell _____

Using an Apostrophe to Show an Omission in a Contraction

Apostrophes are used to show omitted letters in contractions, such as *don't* (*do not*) or *isn't* (*is not*). Contractions are commonly used in informal writing but are usually omitted from formal writing, such as research papers, business letters, and legal documents. You should check with your teacher to see if contractions are acceptable in your writing assignments. Here are some common contractions:

cannot	can't
could have	could've
could not	couldn't
did not	didn't
do not	don't
has not	hasn't
have not	haven't

he is	he's
he would	he'd
I am	I'm
I would	I'd
it is	it's
let us	let's
she is	she's
she will	she'll
should have	should've
should not	shouldn't
they are	they're
they are not	they aren't
was not	wasn't
who is	who's
will not	won't
would have	would've
would not	wouldn't

In speech, we can hear these contractions. What we cannot hear is exactly where the apostrophe goes—where the letter was actually omitted.

wouldn't, *not* would'nt   **(The apostrophe marks the omission of the o in *not*.)**

they're, *not* theyr'e   **(The apostrophe marks the omission of the a in *are*.)**

Remember to put the apostrophe exactly where the letter is missing.

Other Uses of the Apostrophe

Use an apostrophe to indicate special uses of time

Incorrect:	It required a year time.
Correct:	It required a year's time.
Incorrect:	We devoted two weeks work to the project.
Correct:	We devoted two weeks' work to the project.

Use an apostrophe to create the plural of numbers mentioned as numbers and letters mentioned as letters

Incorrect:	You forgot to add the 4s and the 6s.
Correct:	You forgot to add the 4's and the 6's.
Incorrect:	Why did you underline all of the bs?
Correct:	Why did you underline all of the b's?

USAGE MONITOR

can't hardly

Avoid this phrase because it is a double negative and therefore poor English: "I *can't hardly* hear you" can easily be replaced with the more refined "I can barely hear you."

Do not use apostrophes unnecessarily

Use an apostrophe only with a possessive.

Incorrect:	The mother's are having a bake sale for Oakton School.
Correct:	The mothers are having a bake sale for Oakton School.

To test whether a noun is possessive or not, turn it into an *of* phrase and see whether it makes sense.

The baby's blanket is wet.	(**baby's blanket** = blanket of the baby = possessive)
The answers' are on the sheet.	(**answers' are** = are of the answers = makes no sense; therefore, not possessive, no apostrophe needed)

Do not use apostrophes with the pronouns his, hers, its, ours, yours, or theirs

Incorrect:	The scarf is hers'.
Correct:	The scarf is hers.
Incorrect:	Put the CD back in it's case.
Correct:	Put the CD back in its case.

It's is a contraction—short for *it is*. If you unravel the contraction, you get

Put the CD back in *it is* case,

which makes no sense.

PRACTICE 2

Rewrite the following sentences to use contractions whenever possible.

Example: They did not obey the rules.

They didn't obey the rules.

1. You should not Rollerblade without knee pads.

_____

_____

2. I could not have cared less.

_____

_____

3. Lou will not take out the garbage.

_____

_____

4. He was not at all impressed with their answer.

_____

_____

5. They said they had not seen him.

_____

_____

6. If he could have attended the meeting, he would have.

_____

_____

7. Why have you not finished your homework?

_____

_____

8. If you did not owe me $10, I would not be so skeptical.

_____

_____

9. I am afraid it is too late for apologies.

_____

_____

10. Who is going to carry in the cake?

_____

_____

PRACTICE 3

Insert apostrophes where needed.

1. Despite health warnings, peoples desire for junk food continues.
2. Were wondering how long hes going to defy the law.
3. According to him, its someone elses fault.
4. Ten artists are displaying their paintings at John Kellers new gallery.

5. Shes afraid of lightning, but he isnt.

6. Africas wildlife attracts many photographers.

7. The storys ending puzzled many readers.

8. My cousin inherited Aunt Idas old piano.

9. The governments leaders would meet only in neutral territory.

10. Marv never crosses his ts.

PRACTICE 4

Every sentence below has one apostrophe error. It may be a missing apostrophe (or 's) in a possessive, a missing apostrophe in a contraction, or an unnecessary apostrophe. Add apostrophes (or 's) where they are needed, and take out all unnecessary apostrophes.

1. Lets fetch Grandpa's coat so he won't be cold.

2. Wasn't he the biggest coward youve ever seen?

3. Put the trophy in it's place on the mantle.

4. Don't be so sure that the bracelet is her's.

5. The contract is asking for a weeks vacation per year.

6. Put an apple and two cookies's in his lunch box.

7. It's my opinion that students should'nt get an *A* on a late paper.

8. The Rodmans' and the Joneses attended the game.

9. Its not up to me to give you a pass.

10. Most of the actors faces had been made up to look old.

Error 15 Review

The passage that follows contains 10 misplaced or missing apostrophes. Rewrite the passage to correct these errors.

> The best taste in the world is that of chocolate. Whether dark cocoa or light milk chocolate, it's creamy texture delights my palate. But chocolate is addictive, and once I start eating it, I ca'nt stop. Lately Ive read that doctors attitudes have changed toward chocolate. Doctors used to warn that chocolate causes tooth decay, headache's, and all manner of other illnesses. But now some medical researchers have found that chocolate is a mood lifter and even an aphrodisiac. I think it was my mothers fudge that started me on the road to becoming a chocoholic. No one elses fudge could compare with her's. I used to sit in my room with a large square of Mom's fudge on a porcelain saucer, and I felt so comforted and queenly as I bit into one nutty piece after another. You woul'dve thought I was in heaven. Other desserts are lovely, but they just dont compare with good chocolate.

_____

_____

_____

_____

_____

_____

_____

_____

_____

_____

To check your progress in meeting this chapter's objectives, log in to **www.mywritinglab.com,** go to the **Study Plan** tab, click on **The 20 Most Common Sentence Errors** and choose **Apostrophes** from the list of subtopics. Read and view the resources in the **Review Materials** section, and then complete the **Recall, Apply,** and **Write** sets in the **Activities** section.

16 Trouble with Quotation Marks

www.CartoonStock.com

"Please stop doing that annoying quote marks thing."

Learning Objective

• Understand the proper use of quotation marks and how they are used with other punctuation

Your ear may tell you when a pause needs a comma, but sometimes your ear is of little use in identifying any other punctuation that's needed. For certain punctuation marks, you must simply learn the rules. In this section you will learn how to use quotation marks correctly.

Using Quotation Marks to Indicate a Person's Exact Words

One of the two main uses for quotation marks (" ") is to indicate a person's exact words—called a direct quotation. Direct quotations can be recorded in a number of different ways, all of which require quotation marks.

> He remarked, "This is rather difficult."
>
> "This is rather difficult," he remarked.
>
> "This," he said, "is rather difficult."
>
> "This is rather difficult," he remarked. "And it doesn't get any easier."

Begin every quotation with a capital letter

Do not, however, use a capital letter for the second part of a divided quotation that is *not* a full sentence:

> "I work at the zoo," she said, "because I love animals."

Here, the second part of the divided quotation is not a full sentence, so although a comma is still used after *said,* the second part of the quotation does not begin with a capital letter.

> "Give her the money," his father said. "She'll put it in the bank for you."

Here the second part of the divided quotation is a full sentence. A period follows *said* and the second part of the quotation begins with a capital letter.

Do not use quotation marks in indirect quotations

An indirect quotation—rewording what someone has said—does not require quotation marks. Often an indirect quotation is announced by the words *that, what,* or *if.* Some examples follow.

Direct quotation:	Peter said, "Go ahead and start without me."
Indirect quotation:	Peter said that we should go ahead and start without him.
Direct quotation:	The butler asked, "Shall I serve tea, Madam?"
Indirect quotation:	The butler asked whether he should serve tea.

PRACTICE 1

Add the required quotation marks.

Example: I'm betting on your horse, said the gambler, because he's the fastest.

> "I'm betting on your horse," said the gambler, "because he's the fastest."

1. Whatever you do, don't look back, said the guide.

2. I'm a man of the ocean, said the sailor. That's why I hate land.

3. Why was I ever born? the teenager asked.

4. To do the dishes, his mother replied. That's why you were born.

5. Alexander wondered, Where have all the flowers gone?

6. I do not, she said, always fall asleep during the sermon.

7. I don't eat anything with eyes, explained the vegetarian.

8. Jumping through the hoop, the tiger seemed to be saying, I'm tired of this.

9. I shower only on Sundays, the old gentleman remarked. I never shower on Mondays.

10. The auctioneer cried, Going, going, gone!

PRACTICE 2

Place quotation marks around the exact words of the speaker; leave the sentence unchanged if the quotation is indirect.

1. John wondered what had happened at the party.

2. Let me guess, Josephine said. You must be the new mail carrier.

3. Tony asked his editor if she had gone crazy.

4. As a matter of fact, the editor replied, I have—from deadlines.

5. The police recommended that we file a report.

6. Happy birthday, we all shouted, and many happy returns.

7. She suggested that we stay for cake and coffee.

8. Walter explained that only one replacement would be hired.

9. Are you here to apply for the job? he asked. Please fill out this application.

10. It's getting late, she said. Are you nearly finished?

Using other punctuation with quotation marks

Commas and periods always go inside quotation marks.

> "The food is very spicy," said Hal.
>
> "Eat slowly," she suggested, "and drink plenty of water."

Question marks and exclamation points go either inside or outside, depending on the sentence.

Inside: "Why are you asking?" the lawyer wondered.

Outside: Who just asked, "Why are you asking"?

In the first example, the spoken words make up a separate question; in the second example, the spoken words are part of the question.

Inside: "Duck!" Paul screamed.

Outside: Stop humming "If Ever I Loved You"!

In the first example, the spoken words make up a separate command; in the second, the spoken words are part of the command.

PRACTICE 3

The sentences that follow use other punctuation marks in connection with quotation marks. In the spaces provided, write *C* if the sentence is correctly punctuated and *NC* if it is not. Correct the sentence if it is incorrectly punctuated.

Example: *C* "What are you doing?" he asked.

1. _____ The acrobat cried, "I missed you"!

2. _____ "How much is your rent?" he asked.

3. _____ The gentleman grumped, "So you say", adding, "but I know better."

4. _____ Who said, "Give me liberty, or give me death"?

5. _____ "Find yourself a job,"! she bawled.

6. _____ "Give me a break!" he cried.

7. _____ Who just said, "I'm tired of this movie?"

8. _____ "Sir," she remarked bitterly, "you are no gentleman".

9. _____ "I will not"! she snapped.

10. _____ They asked, "Now, what's the matter"?

Using Quotation Marks to Indicate the Titles of Short Works

Use quotation marks to indicate the titles of short works such as newspaper or magazine articles, poems, songs, and short stories.

Underline or italicize the titles of long works

Use underlining or italics to indicate the titles of long works such as books, movies, magazines, plays, television shows, record albums, and CDs.

SHORTER WORKS	LONGER WORKS
Magazine article—"Outlet Shopping"	Magazine—*Consumer Reports*
Newspaper article—"City Council Approves New Train Station"	Newspaper—*The Cleveland Press*
Book chapter—"The Child from Ages 2 to 6"	Book—*Child Development*
Poem—"America"	Poetry collection—*The Collected Poems of Allen Ginsberg*
Song—"Buffalo Soldier"	Movie—*Shane*
Editorial—"Stand Up for Your Rights"	Television series—*Frasier*
	CD—*Mary Stallings: Fine and Mellow*

PRACTICE 4

Add quotation marks or underlining as required.

Example: Stay Young is an essay that appears in an anthology entitled Readings for Writers.

"Stay Young" is an essay that appears in an anthology entitled <u>Readings for Writers</u>.

1. Chapter 3 is entitled Purpose and Thesis.

2. My favorite Bob Marley song is No Woman No Cry.

3. Running in the Family is an amusing book.

4. My uncle's favorite book is A Passage to India.

5. Did you see the movie Titanic?

6. I read an interesting editorial in the Atlanta Constitution; it was called Enough Already.

7. The Jamaica Journal is an informative magazine about Jamaica.

8. I love the television series The Nanny.

9. Saving Private Ryan is a realistic but gory movie.

10. His favorite play is Death of a Salesman.

Error 16 Review

Add quotation marks or underlining where needed.

My aunt and I have a private book club. Every week, we try to read a book together and then discuss it afterward. Sometimes we choose a book that's too big to be read in a week, and it takes us longer. The last book we read together was The Nightmare Years by William L. Shirer. My aunt's favorite chapter in that book is Chapter 4, which is entitled The Year Off in Spain, 1933. I like the way he writes, said my aunt. I especially like his plain style. Yes, yes, yes, I replied, he gets right into his subject quickly and without any fussiness. What do you mean by fussiness? my aunt wondered. I explained that I meant Shirer is not a pretentious writer. He's always down-to-earth and to the point, I added. My aunt agreed with me. She said she found that trait also in his most famous book, The Rise and Fall of the Third Reich, which we read last year. He writes that way, said my aunt, because he used to be a newspaper reporter for the Chicago Tribune. He learned his writing trade in the newsroom. When we're finished reading this book, we intend to read Berlin Diary, Stranger Come Home, and The Rise and Fall of Adolf Hitler, which are other books by Mr. Shirer.

To check your progress in meeting this chapter's objectives, log in to **www.mywritinglab.com,** go to the **Study Plan** tab, click on **The 20 Most Common Sentence Errors** and choose **Quotation Marks** from the list of subtopics. Read and view the resources in the **Review Materials** section, and then complete the **Recall, Apply,** and **Write** sets in the **Activities** section.

17 Incorrect Capitalization, Part I

Because capital (uppercase) and lowercase letters sound the same, your ear cannot help you with capitalization. *Penny,* the name, sounds the same as *penny,* the noun that means "a one-cent coin." To learn capitalization, you must know the rules. Here are some rules (you will learn additional rules in the next section, Error 18):

Learning Objective

- Understand and follow the rules of capitalization

- Capitalize the first word in a sentence or direct quotation.

- Capitalize names of individual persons and the word *I.*

- Capitalize family relationships used as names.

- Capitalize the names of nationalities, religions, races, tribes, and languages.

- Capitalize the first word after a colon if what follows the colon is a full sentence.

- Capitalize the names of the days of the week, months of the year, holidays, and religious occasions.

- Capitalize the names of specific places, including monuments.

- Capitalize the names of companies, clubs, political groups, and other official organizations.

We will look at each rule of capitalization in turn.

Capitalize the first word in a sentence or direct quotation

Children often feel insecure.

Ralph Sockman said, "The test of courage comes when we are in the minority; the test of tolerance comes when we are in the majority."

"The fault," she insisted, "is in us."

Notice that in the third example, *The* is capitalized because it begins a new sentence; however, *is* remains lowercase because it a continuation of the first part of the sentence.

179

PRACTICE 1

Correctly capitalize the following sentences.

1. Jessica complained vigorously. she said she felt deprived.

2. "can you give me a map?" she asked. "my sense of direction is terrible."

3. Carmen laughed, "he'll be fine if you just leave him alone."

4. I want to be remembered as a helpful person. helpful people are saints.

5. Run for your life! don't stay under the tree.

Capitalize names of individuals and the word *I*

> Give the note to Ginny Ehrlich, not to Fred Douglas.
>
> Our family doctor is Ruth Kazan.
>
> He repeated the question so that I would hear it.

Nicknames are also capitalized.

> He was known by his buddies as Big Shoulder Beans.

PRACTICE 2

Capitalize the names of individuals in the following sentences.

1. All Americans revere abraham lincoln.

2. I hate it when my dad's college pals call him shorty.

3. Laurence Bradley, Carolyn costaldo, and jose gutierrez are scheduled to talk at Career Day.

4. The greatest Sioux leader was sitting bull.

5. Many cities have named streets after the great civil rights leader martin luther king.

Capitalize family relationships used as names

> Here comes Uncle Joe, drunk as a lord.
>
> After Grandpa Justin had lunch, we went to the park.
>
> Please don't give Mom so much trouble.

Note that you do not capitalize *mother, father, grandmother, grandfather, uncle, aunt, cousin,* and so forth when these terms are preceded by *my, your, our,* or any other possessive word.

> Ask Grandma if she'd like more tea.
>
> but
>
> Ask your grandma if she'd like more tea.

His aunt raises golden retrievers.

but

Auntie Meg raises golden retrievers.

PRACTICE 3

Capitalize wherever necessary. Write *C* in the blank if the sentence is correct.

1. ____ My mother grew up on a farm in West Texas.

2. ____ I was so mortified that I never wanted to see aunt Ruby again.

3. ____ Her grandmother could ride a horse like a cowboy in a rodeo.

4. ____ My uncle Frank never mentions his brother, Norm.

5. ____ If you take dad to the airport, remind him to call mom.

Capitalize the names of nationalities, religions, races, tribes, and languages

I love Chinese, Vietnamese, and Italian food.

The Baptist, Methodist, and Catholic churches are sponsoring a community picnic on Sunday.

Denise Chavez writes about the Mexican-American community in New Mexico.

Native Americans of the Southwest include the Zunis, Navajos, Apaches, and Utes.

Most people in Montreal speak both French and English.

PRACTICE 4

Fill in the blanks as indicated.

Example: In high school, I took (language) _Spanish_.

1. My best friend is (nationality) _____.

2. Someone who is bilingual speaks two languages fluently, such as _____ and _____.

3. People who live in Canada are _____, and people who live in Mexico are _____.

4. There are many Protestant denominations, including _____, _____, and _____.

5. The (races) _____, _____, and _____ must learn to appreciate one another's cultures.

Capitalize the first word after a colon if what follows is a full sentence

Here is a command I can respect: "Love your neighbor as yourself."

but

The following ingredients are needed: eggs, flour, sugar, and milk.

PRACTICE 5

If a sentence is capitalized correctly, leave it alone. If it is not correct, write a capital letter above any lowercase letter that should be capitalized.

Example: Dear Sir: We regret that the table you ordered is still not in stock.

1. Please enclose the following papers: the bank statement, the tax return, and the application.

2. The poem begins as follows: "despair is a snake with black wings."

3. Follow these directions: dig a trench, hammer some stakes into the ground, and set up the tent.

4. Here are the virtues I am anticipating: loyalty, courage, and faith.

5. This is what I advised him: continue to take your medicine and see what happens.

Capitalize the days of the week, months of the year, holidays, and religious occasions

Labor Day always falls on a Monday.

My favorite time to ski is in January or February.

Halloween is a very popular holiday.

Every Easter, I attend church services at sunrise.

Note that the seasons of the year are not capitalized:

I love fall, when all the leaves take on brilliant hues.

In the spring, people's thoughts turn to love.

PRACTICE 6

In the spaces provided, mark *C* if the sentence is properly capitalized and *NC* if it is not. Then correct the errors.

1. _____ Many Americans celebrate palm sunday as well as passover.

2. _____ Next Summer I plan to visit Guadalajara.

3. _____ I attend night school on tuesdays and wednesdays.

4. _____ Does school close on Martin Luther King Day?

5. _____ Every Christmas I eat candy until I'm sick.

Capitalize the names of specific places, including monuments

Last summer we visited Mount Rushmore.

Someday I want to visit the Leaning Tower of Pisa in Italy.

Who engineered the Golden Gate Bridge?

I attend New York University and hope to graduate this year.

Follow Anderson Blvd. all the way to Stocker Road.

Park right in front of Brown's Bakery Shop.

Do not capitalize the names of places that are not specific.

He walked down the street toward the bakery shop.

but

He walked down Maple Street to Brown's Bakery Shop.

PRACTICE 7

Correct the capitalization errors in these sentences.

1. The hurricane hit miami and tampa before heading up the coast to south carolina.

2. Thousands of people visit yellowstone national park and mount rushmore each year.

3. My mother was born in the small town of haskell, texas; my father came from limerick, ireland.

4. First I have to stop at wagner's drug store and then at five star cleaners, which is right next door.

5. New orleans is on lake pontchartrain, which empties into the gulf of mexico.

Capitalize the names of companies, clubs, political groups, and other official organizations

You can still get "full service" at some Standard Oil stations.

"Bonjour" is the name of our French Club.

My brother switched from the Republican Party to the Democratic Party.

I belong to the National Organization for Women.

The Federal Bureau of Investigation (FBI) is headquartered in Washington.

PRACTICE 8

Underline the words that should be capitalized in the following sentences.

1. Our college uses national-international student programs (NISP) for its international study programs.

2. Belonging to the sorority alpha sigma alpha has helped me make friends on campus.

3. Several of my friends work at pacific bell telephone company.

4. Our next-door neighbor has been elected to the house of representatives.

5. She works at flossmore general hospital.

Error 17 Review

Correct all the capitalization errors in the following essay.

I love santa fe, new mexico. When you drive through the center of town, you would never guess that this is a state capital. The small town square is bordered on all sides by fabulous shops displaying authentic indian jewelry, rugs, and pottery. At the center of the square is a pretty little park where you can watch tribal dances and listen to hispanic music. One side of the square is called governor's mansion. Along its front is a shopping area, where craftspeople from the various pueblos of the area display their wares. They sell hopi kachina dolls, zuni fetishes, navajo silver jewelry, and acoma pots. When I visit santa fe, I always stop by the wheelwright museum because it has a wonderful gift shop where I can buy antique hopi kachinas. I also love to drive out to the little town of susuque for some delicious mexican tamales, smothered in red salsa and accompanied by freshly mashed guacamole. There's a picturesque little catholic church with a classic black steeple standing at the side of the road. If I have the time, I like to hike in bandolier national monument or take a drive to some of the famous rock formations, like ship rock or camel rock. Because all houses in santa fe are made of adobe, you might think you're in some mexican village when you drive up hyde park road toward the ski lift. The new mexico sky in santa fe is gorgeous—filled with giant white, puffy clouds that are a magical backdrop for lightning storms at night. Santa fe may not be as wild and exciting as chicago or new york city, but it is stunning in its artistic charms.

To check your progress in meeting this chapter's objectives, log in to **www.mywritinglab.com,** go to the **Study Plan** tab, click on **The 20 Most Common Sentence Errors** and choose **Capitalization** from the list of subtopics. Read and view the resources in the **Review Materials** section, and then complete the **Recall, Apply,** and **Write** sets in the **Activities** section.

ERROR

18 INCORRECT CAPITALIZATION, PART II

I n the previous section, Error 17, you learned these rules for capitalizing correctly:

Learning Objective

- Understand additional rules of capitalization

- Capitalize the first word in a sentence or direct quotation.

- Capitalize names of individual persons and the word *I*.

- Capitalize family relationships used as names.

- Capitalize the names of nationalities, religions, races, tribes, and languages.

- Capitalize the first word after a colon if what follows is a full sentence.

- Capitalize the names of the days of the week, months of the year, holidays, and religious occasions.

- Capitalize the names of specific places, including monuments.

- Capitalize the names of companies, clubs, political groups, and other official organizations.

Now you will learn these additional capitalization rules:

- Capitalize the names of commercial products.

- Capitalize titles of books, magazines, newspapers, essays, poems, stories, plays, articles, films, television shows, songs, CDs, and cartoons.

- Capitalize titles used in front of a person's name.

- Capitalize specific college courses but not general courses.

- Capitalize areas of the country.

- Capitalize historical eras and events.

- Capitalize abbreviations of familiar organizations, corporations, people, countries, time, and titles.

- Capitalize the opening and the first word of the closing of a letter.

Capitalize the names of commercial products

I use Tide because it works as well as any other laundry detergent.

Do not capitalize types of products.

We need paper towels, spaghetti sauce, and peanut butter.	**(These are merely types of products, not brand names.)**

but

That Post oatmeal is good.	(***Post* is a brand name, but *oatmeal* is a type of food.)**

PRACTICE 1

Capitalize the names of commercial products in the following sentences.

1. _____ I love hershey's chocolate.

2. _____ My favorite milk additive is carnation.

3. _____ I always use gillette shaving cream.

4. _____ The most popular car of the 1960s was the volkswagen.

5. _____ To repel mosquitoes, off works really well.

Capitalize titles of books, magazines, newspapers, essays, poems, stories, plays, articles, films, television shows, songs, CDs, and cartoons

Book:	Have you read *Hearts* by Hilma Wolitzer?
Magazine:	I subscribe to *Discover* magazine.
Newspaper:	*The Washington Post* is a respected newspaper.
Essay:	Her essay is entitled "Affirmative Action and Women: Off the Cuff Comments."
Poem:	I love Lorena Bruff's poem "The Cello."
Story:	"A Worn Path" is a moving short story.
Play:	She was wonderful in *King Lear*.
Article:	Read the article called "Shakespeare in the Bush."
Film:	*Civil Action* is a powerful movie.
Television Show:	I always watch *60 Minutes* on Sunday night.
Song:	Bob Marley's "War" uses the words of a speech as its lyrics.
CD:	When I'm tired, I listen to *Andrea Bocelli: Sogno*, a CD full of comforting music.
Cartoon:	I miss *The Far Side* cartoons.

Notice how words are capitalized in titles. The beginning word is always capitalized. The first word after a colon is also always capitalized. Certain words are not capitalized, however, unless they come at the beginning of the title.

Do not capitalize:

- An article (*a, an,* or *the*) unless it is the first word.

- The coordinating conjunctions *and, but, yet, or, nor, so,* and *for.*

- Short prepositions such as *of, from, by, in, up,* and *out* (but do capitalize prepositions of five or more letters, such as *about, among, between, behind, through, though,* and *without*).

PRACTICE 2

Correctly capitalize the titles in the following sentences.

1. I read an article in *science fiction digest* entitled "UFOs appear in farmer's field."

---

2. Paul Laurence Dunbar wrote a poem called "we wear the mask."

---

3. Two of my favorite television shows are *wheel of fortune* and *mad about you.*

---

4. "The snows of kilimanjaro" can be found in the book *collected short stories of ernest hemingway.*

---

5. First she sang "fly me to the moon" and then "moon over Miami."

Capitalize titles used in front of a person's name

President Barack Obama, Governor Charlie Crist, Secretary of State Hillary Clinton, General David H. Petraeus, Attorney General Eric H. Holder, Mrs. Miller, Mr. Planter, Ms. Lowery

but

Barack Obama, the president of the United States; Charlie Crist, the governor of Georgia; Hillary Clinton, secretary of state; David H. Petraeus, general; Eric H. Holder, attorney general of the United States

PRACTICE 3

In the blank in front of each sentence, write *C* if the sentence is correct and *NC* if it is incorrect. If it is incorrect, write the correction above the incorrect word.

1. ___ Warren Christopher was once the Secretary of State.

2. ___ My congratulations to Mr. Smith and miss james.

3. ____ One day a woman will be President of the United States.

4. ____ Richard Nixon was once vice president of the United States.

5. ____ They said that Congresswoman McKinney would speak.

Capitalize specific college courses but not general courses

I aced the exam in Algebra 100.

but

All my life I've hated algebra.

I am taking Introduction to Psychology.

but

Classes in psychology are very popular.

Language courses are always capitalized

I'm taking French 100.

I'm planning on studying Chinese.

USAGE MONITOR

Academic subjects

As a college student, you should observe these three rules when using the names of academic subjects in your writing:

1. General names of subjects, such as *history, economics, geography, mechanical engineering,* or *law,* are NOT capitalized.

2. Individual courses, such as *Economics 101, Art Appreciation 115,* or *Bible as Literature,* are capitalized.

3. The names of specific departments, such as *Department of African Studies, Geography Department,* or *Department of Sciences,* are capitalized.

PRACTICE 4

Correct all capitalization errors by using the upper- or lowercase where necessary. Remember to capitalize the names of specific college courses.

1. The hardest class I ever took was organic chemistry.

2. Last semester I got an *A* in anthropology and a *B* in Spanish.

3. This afternoon, I shall stop by the office of foreign languages.

4. He says he is taking religion 101.

5. Why do you like Geometry better than Physics?

6. I made a fool of myself in Professor Boyle's basic ballet steps class.

7. My community college offers a class titled "advanced signing for the hearing impaired."

8. If we don't learn from History, how can we improve our future?

9. All Engineering Classes are housed in a temporary building situated near the Quad.

10. Cleaning Oil Spills 101 is a class someone should invent.

Capitalize areas of the country

People in the Midwest sometimes talk like Canadians.

We decided to move to the South.

I'll never live on the West Coast.

Do not capitalize compass directions or areas of the country used as adjectives.

Go south for two blocks, then turn north.

My mother speaks with a western twang.

PRACTICE 5

Fill in the blanks with an area of the country or a compass direction. Be sure to capitalize correctly.

Example: Her favorite aunt lives on the <u>East Coast</u>.

1. On the _____ side of the mountains was a valley.

2. We drove all night, always heading _____.

3. Thirteen years ago I moved from the _____ Coast to the _____ Coast.

4. If I could choose, I'd live in the _____.

5. Go _____ on Berkford, and then turn _____ on Nancy Creek.

Capitalize historical eras and events

In the Age of Reason, humans tried to make sense of their world.

I wish I had lived during the Medieval Period.

Poetry from the Romantic Age is largely about nature.

Many Americans were hurt during the Depression.

The Battle of the Bulge was the last great battle of World War II.

PRACTICE 6

In each pair below, mark *C* beside the sentence that is correctly capitalized.

1. ____ **(a).** Custer was killed in the battle of little big horn.

   ____ **(b).** Custer was killed in the Battle of Little Big Horn.

2. ____ **(a).** The Civil War pitted American against American.

   ____ **(b).** The civil war pitted American against American.

3. ____ **(a).** In the Victorian age, people were very prudish.

   ____ **(b).** In the Victorian Age, people were very prudish.

4. ____ **(a).** The modern age is characterized by many good novels.

   ____ **(b).** The Modern Age is characterized by many good novels.

5. ____ **(a).** World War I was settled by the Treaty of Versailles.

   ____ **(b).** World war I was settled by the treaty of versailles.

Capitalize abbreviations of familiar organizations, corporations, people, countries, time, and titles

Organizations:	FAA, NCAA, MADD, AEC
Corporations:	GE, AT&T, MCI, IBM, AOL
People:	JFK, FDR, LBJ
Countries:	U.S.A. *or* USA, U.K. *or* UK
Time:	12:00 A.M., 2:30 P.M.
Titles:	Benjamin Stein, Sr.; Felicia Baquero, M.D.; Theodore Munch, Ph.D.; Carolyn Wu, D.D.S.

USAGE MONITOR

Although social networks are still too new to have been assigned capitalization rules in grammar books, the majority of them are capitalized as follows: Facebook, Twitter, YouTube, MySpace, Linkedin, Meetup, and so forth. For the sake of simplicity, they are spelled the way their creators spell them.

PRACTICE 7

Complete the following sentences with the appropriate abbreviations.

1. The abbreviation for the Soviet Union was _____.

2. The Boy Scouts of America is sometimes abbreviated _____.

3. The Food and Drug Administration, or _____, is an important government agency.

4. Alcoholics Anonymous is known as _____, and the Automobile Association of American is known as _____.

5. John Chavez is both a medical doctor, or _____, and a doctor of philosophy, or _____.

Capitalize the opening and the first word of the closing of a letter

Dear Madame,

My dear Joseph,

Dear Dr. Pevitts,

Sincerely,

Sincerely yours,

Best regards,

Love and kisses,

PRACTICE 8

Write a letter about yourself as part of a college application. Capitalize correctly.

Error 18 Review

Correct all the capitalization errors in the following letter.

april 1, 2008

Dear Peter,

this is a hard letter to write because I do not convey bad news well. I have signed up for three classes, all of which I like. I'm enrolled in introduction to freshman composition, economics 101, and us history from the revolutionary war to the civil war. I expect to do well in all of them because I am determined to study hard and get good grades. What's the bad news? Well, it is this: the girl you like so much—the one from the south who speaks in such a charming way—is in all my classes. What's more, on her own and without any prompting whatsoever from me, she has decided to sit right next to me in every class. I told her that you would not like that, especially since you come from the northeast and have a very jealous nature. You know what she said? She said she doesn't care if you are secretly a cia agent from Washington, d.c.; she intends to sit where she pleases. What can I do? I'm just a kid from the west coast who is used to free-spirited california girls. I told you that you should've stayed at citrus college rather than transfer to riverside university, but you wouldn't listen. Now, because of your thoughtlessness, I'm stuck with the prettiest girl in town.

yours sincerely,

John

P.S. I don't work for the fbi, but this is a fib. Happy april fool's day!

To check your progress in meeting this chapter's objectives, log in to **www.mywritinglab.com,** go to the **Study Plan** tab, click on **The 20 Most Common Sentence Errors** and choose **Capitalization** from the list of subtopics. Read and view the resources in the **Review Materials** section, and then complete the **Recall, Apply,** and **Write** sets in the **Activities** section.

www.CartoonStock.com

Learning Objective

- Understand the rules for spelling in different tenses and learn tips for improving spelling

Before the existence of dictionaries, words were spelled entirely by ear or according to the writer's whim. For example, *slow* might have been spelled *sloe, slo,* or *slough.* With the appearance in the 18th century of the first English dictionary, however, spelling gradually became standardized to the point that children today compete in spelling bees.

Even if we never get skilled enough at spelling to be able to enter a spelling bee, we can all become better spellers by observing some simple rules.

Tips for Improving Your Spelling

1. Sound out words. For instance, you will be able to identify that the word *government* contains an *n* if you say it aloud slowly. The word *find* has a final "d" sound and should not be spelled *fine*. Here are other words that need sounding out:

   accidentally (not "accidently"), *athlete* (not "atholete"), *candidate* (not "candate"), *February* (not "Febuary"), *generally* (not "genrally"), *height* (not "heighth"), *nuclear* (not "nucular"), *perspire* (not "pespire"), *realtor* (not "realator"), *strength* (not "strenth"), *supposed* (not "suppose")

   Words like *and, than,* and *have* are often slurred in speech and therefore misspelled.

   Incorrect:　I would of expected pie for dessert rather then fruit an cheese.

   Correct:　I would have expected pie for dessert rather than fruit and cheese.

   Reading a word aloud can definitely help you to spell it correctly.

2. Make up your own memory tricks for remembering the spelling of problem words. For example, *cemetery* is spelled with all *e*'s because it is so eerie; the *principal* is your pal; *dessert* has two *s*'s because it is doubly good.

3. Use a dictionary. Looking up words regularly will help you become familiar with any quirks in their spellings. Ask your teacher to recommend a good dictionary.

4. Keep a list of words you often misspell and refer to it when you proofread your writing.

5. If you write using a computer, the first rule of spelling is simply this: Use the spell checker that comes with your writing program. Most programs have spell checkers built into them. However, even sophisticated spell checkers go only so far. Although they catch such misspellings as *heighth* for *height* and *occassion* for *occasion,* they won't tell you if you've incorrectly used *its* for *it's* or *their* for *there* or *they're.* So be sure to proofread your writing carefully before turning it in.

Rules for Spelling

Spelling in English is not always as clear-cut as we would like. Nearly every rule has an exception. Nevertheless, learning the rules and their exceptions will make you a better speller.

As you go over the rules, bear in mind the difference between vowels and consonants.

Vowels:　　　　*a, e, i, o, u,* and sometimes *y*

Consonants:　　all other letters of the alphabet

Using *ie* and *ei*

Remember the age-old rule: "*i* before *e* except after *c* or when sounded like *ay* as in *neighbor* or *weigh*."

niece

relieve

believe

but

ceiling

receive

deceive

EXCEPTIONS		
either	leisure	species
caffeine	neither	their
financier	seize	weird
foreigner	science	
height	society	

PRACTICE 1

Underline the correct spelling in each pair of words in parentheses.

1. (Neither, Niether) Fred nor Mark is going to the club brunch.

2. They bought (their, thier) tickets in advance.

3. What is that (wierd, weird) sound?

4. A good (neighbor, nieghbor) is as valuable as silver or gold.

5. What do you like to do in your (leisure, liesure) time?

6. Drinks that contain salt are just as bad as those that contain (caffeine, caffiene).

7. You cannot live a serene life if you flout the rules of (soceity, society).

8. She has always done well in (sceince, science) courses.

9. If you (believe, beleive) that, I have a bridge to sell you.

10. She left a (breif, brief) e-mail message for me.

Changing *y* to *i*

When you add an ending to a word that ends in a consonant plus *y,* change the *y* to *i*. Keep the final *y* when it is preceded by a vowel.

try + ed = tried

worry + er = worrier

silly + ness = silliness

buy + er = buyer

sway + ing = swaying

EXCEPTIONS	
horrify	horrifying
lady	ladylike
carry	carrying
cry	crying (*but* crier)
worry	worrying
study	studying

PRACTICE 2

Combine the following words with the ending shown and place the correct word in the blank provided.

Example: study + es = studies

1. testify	+	es	=	_____
2. merry	+	ly	=	_____
3. muddy	+	ed	=	_____
4. mortify	+	es	=	_____
5. lazy	+	ly	=	_____
6. bury	+	ing	=	_____
7. obey	+	ing	=	_____
8. fry	+	ed	=	_____
9. lonely	+	ness	=	_____
10. beauty	+	ful	=	_____

The silent final *e*

When you add an ending that starts with a vowel, such as *-al, -able, -ence,* or *-ing,* drop the final *e* from the main word. When you add an ending that starts with a consonant, such as *-ment, -less,* or *-ly,* keep the final *e.*

Here are some examples for you to study:

bride	+	al	=	bridal
like	+	able	=	likable
emerge	+	ence	=	emergence
take	+	ing	=	taking

manage	+	ment	=	management
love	+	less	=	loveless
polite	+	ly	=	politely

EXCEPTIONS

argue	+	ment	=	argument
courage	+	ous	=	courageous
judge	+	ment	=	judgment
manage	+	able	=	manageable
nine	+	th	=	ninth
notice	+	able	=	noticeable
true	+	ly	=	truly

PRACTICE 3

Place a *C* to the left of each word that is spelled correctly.

Example: _____ pleasureable __*C*__ pleasurable

1. _____ likeable _____ likable
2. _____ management _____ managment
3. _____ desperately _____ desperatly
4. _____ arguement _____ argument
5. _____ dosage _____ doseage
6. _____ movable _____ moveable
7. _____ managing _____ manageing
8. _____ useable _____ usable
9. _____ judgement _____ judgment
10. _____ supposing _____ supposeing

Doubling the final consonant

In one-syllable words

To add -*ed*, -*ing*, -*er*, or -*est* to a one-syllable word, double the consonant of the word if it is preceded by a single vowel.

pin	+	ed	=	pinned
trim	+	ing	=	trimming
thin	+	er	=	thinner
sad	+	est	=	saddest

PRACTICE 4

Add the indicated endings to the words listed below and spell them correctly in the blanks provided.

Example: set (ing) <u>setting</u>

1. dip (ed) _____

2. stop (ing) _____

3. dig (ing) _____

4. flop (ed) _____

5. knit (ed) _____

6. run (er) _____

7. slam (ed) _____

8. drop (ing) _____

9. blab (ed) _____

10. big (est) _____

In multisyllable words

To add *-ing* or *-ed* to words of more than one syllable, double the final consonant if the following are true:

- The stress is on the final syllable.

  com-mit′

  be-gin′

  oc-cur′

- The last three letters consist of a consonant/vowel/consonant.

  commit

  begin

  occur

Therefore:

commit	+	ed	=	committed
begin	+	ing	=	beginning
occur	+	ed	=	occurred

Now, consider these words:

travel = traveling	**(Do not double, because the accent is on the first syllable: *tra′-vel.*)**
benefit = benefited	**(Do not double, because the accent is on the first syllable: *ben′-e-fit.*)**
repeat = repeating	**(Do not double, because the last three letters do not fit the consonant/vowel/consonant pattern.)**

PRACTICE 5

In the blanks on the right, add *-ed* and *-ing* to the following words.

	–ED	**–ING**
Example: admit	admitted	admitting
1. prefer	_____	_____
2. unwrap	_____	_____
3. expel	_____	_____
4. remit	_____	_____
5. defer	_____	_____

PRACTICE 6

Add *-ed* and *-ing* to the following words.

1. travel + ed _____ + ing _____

2. suspect + ed _____ + ing _____

3. profit + ed _____ + ing _____

4. label + ed _____ + ing _____

5. defect + ed _____ + ing _____

Forming plurals

Most words plural form their plurals by simply adding *-s*.

SINGULAR	PLURAL
sled	sleds
egg	eggs
sister	sisters
rag	rags

However, there are a few exceptions that you should master.

Words ending in *-s, -ss, -z, -x, -sh,* or *-ch*

Words ending in *-s, -ss, -z, -x, -sh,* or *-ch* form their plurals by adding the extra syllable *-es* for easier pronunciation.

SINGULAR	PLURAL
lens	lenses
kiss	kisses

buzz	buzzes
box	boxes
wash	washes
church	churches

PRACTICE 7

Form the plurals of the following words.

1. fox _____

2. crash _____

3. beach _____

4. buzz _____

5. dash _____

6. mix _____

7. bush _____

8. quiz _____

9. brush_____

10. bus _____

Words ending in -o

If a word ends in an -o preceded by a vowel, add -s:

rodeo	rodeos
patio	patios
zoo	zoos
radio	radios
video	videos

If a word ends in an -o preceded by a consonant, add -es:

hero	heroes
potato	potatoes
echo	echoes
buffalo	buffaloes

EXCEPTIONS

alto	altos
grotto	grottos
memo	memos
motto	mottos
photo	photos
piano	pianos
solo	solos

PRACTICE 8

Write a sentence for each of the following words using the plural form.

1. potato

_____

2. video

_____

3. motto

_____

4. echo

_____

5. radio

_____

6. tomato

_____

7. zoo

_____

8. hero

_____

9. piano

_____

10. solo

_____

Words ending in -f

Most words ending in *-f* (or *-fe*) change the *f* to a *v* and add *-es*.

SINGULAR	PLURAL
half	halves
calf	calves
leaf	leaves
wife	wives

EXCEPTIONS	
roof	roofs
safe	safes
chief	chiefs
proof	proofs

PRACTICE 9

Form the plurals of the following words.

1. leaf _____

2. spoof _____

3. half _____

4. safe _____

5. wharf _____

6. handkerchief _____

7. thief _____

8. knife _____

9. calf _____

10. hoof _____

Irregular plurals

Some words form irregular plurals.

SINGULAR	PLURAL
woman	women
foot	feet
ox	oxen
mouse	mice

PRACTICE 10

Form the plurals of the following words.

1. goose _____

2. man _____

3. child _____

4. louse _____

5. woman _____

Words that do not change

Some words have the same spelling for the singular and plural forms.

SINGULAR	PLURAL
deer	deer
fish	fish (*or* fishes)
sheep	sheep
species	species

series   series

moose   moose

PRACTICE 11

Turn the following words into plurals and then write a sentence using the plural.

Example: deer   <u>deer</u>

<u>We saw a herd of deer at the saltlick.</u>

1. fish _____

_____

2. mouse _____

_____

3. moose _____

_____

4. series _____

_____

5. sheep _____

_____

PRACTICE 12

Circle the word in each pair that is correctly spelled.

1. halfs, halves

2. measurless, measureless

3. admited, admitted

4. expeled, expelled

5. pianos, pianoes

6. refitted, refited

7. mouses, mice

8. biggest, bigest

9. tomatoes, tomatos

10. slopy, sloppy

11. heros, heroes

12. writing, writting

13. likable, likeable

14. permited, permitted

15. occurring, occuring

16. percieve, receive

17. argument, arguement

18. hieght, height

19. coppying, copying

20. wives, wifes

Error 19 Review

Rewrite the following passage to correct all misspelled words (there are 14).

Scuba diving terrifys me. Although I have recieved a diploma admiting me to the elite group of certified scuba divers, I have never conquered my fear when under water. Niether my fearless brother nor my athletic sister has ever been able to releive my nervousness. Once I put on my scuba diving suit and grab my gear in readyness for a diving expedition, all I can think about is getting back home. I don't mind the cold water; I don't mind the tight divving suit. My bigest problem is the foriegn world that greets me under water. For instance, there is the slimmy seaweed brushing against my face and making me afraid that it will start wraping around my neck or around the valves of my oxygen tank. I don't even enjoy seeing the multi-hued fish swiming because I'm so scarred that a shark might be hidden among them. As for the darkness at depths of more than 30 feet, I just want to get back up to the world above the sea waves. Beleive me, I'm always utterly grateful to climb back on board the boat and head back to shore.

_____

_____

_____

_____

_____

_____

_____

_____

To check your progress in meeting this chapter's objectives, log in to **www.mywritinglab.com,** go to the **Study Plan** tab, click on **The 20 Most Common Sentence Errors** and choose **Spelling** from the list of subtopics. Read and view the resources in the **Review Materials** section, and then complete the **Recall, Apply,** and **Write** sets in the **Activities** section.

Learning Objective

- Identify frequently confused words and commonly misspelled words

English spelling is difficult. Words are often not spelled the way they sound. *Raccoon* sounds like it should have a *k* but it doesn't. *Threw* sounds like *through* but is spelled differently. *Though, cough,* and *through* look like rhyming words, but actually are not pronounced at all alike. Given that English has a vocabulary of over 400,000 words, it's a wonder that we spell as well as we do.

Some words—called **homophones**—sound exactly alike but have different spellings and meanings. Other words are not exactly homophones but are similar enough to be confused with each other. Study the following examples:

altar (a raised platform in church)	alter (to change)
it's (it is)	its (pronoun: *Its engine was throbbing.*)
accept (to receive with consent: *They accept our offer.*)	except (exclude: *Everyone cried except Peter.*)
advice (noun: *I gave my advice.*)	advise (verb: *I advise you to leave.*)

Homophones and Frequently Confused Words

Learn the meaning and spelling of the following homophones and frequently confused words. Errors in spelling can change the meaning of writing. *Angel* spelled correctly will still confuse your reader if you really mean *angle*.

accept—to take or receive/**except**—excluding, other than, but for

They accept our thanks.

I work every day except Sunday.

access—a means of approach/**excess**—more than the usual

She had access to my room.

Drinking to excess is not good.

advice—recommendation (noun)/**advise**—to caution, to warn (verb)

The lawyer's advice is to do nothing.

I advise you not to move.

affect—to influence, to change/**effect**—to bring about (verb); consequence, result (noun)

Watching too much television affected my sanity.

The new supervisor effected some good changes.

It will have an effect on my pocketbook.

altar—a raised platform in a church/**alter**—to change

They exchanged wedding vows at the altar.

The coach should alter the pitcher's motion.

bare—without covering or clothing/**bear**—to bring forth, to endure (verb); an animal (noun)

The playing field was bare of any grass.

Every year the mares bear foals.

I can't bear going to the dentist.

As I hiked past the river, I spotted a bear.

capital—value of goods, money; a principal city/**capitol**—a building in which legislators meet

Investors should not squander their capital.

Nashville is the capital of Tennessee.

The capitol was a scene of heated debate.

cite—to quote/**site**—a place or scene/**sight**—ability to see

He loves to cite Shakespeare's words.

The site for the monument was chosen by a committee.

He claims to have the gift of second sight.

course—a path; a subject taken in school/**coarse**—rough in texture

>The obstacle course took us over mountains.

>I'm taking a course in literature.

>The sheets felt coarse.

desert—a dry land (noun); to abandon (verb)/**dessert**—something sweet served at the end of a meal

>We're going to the desert for the weekend.

>Don't desert me at the altar.

>My favorite dessert is strawberry shortcake.

forth—forward/**fourth**—comes after *third*

>The settlers went forth into the wilderness.

>The fourth planet is Mars.

its—possessive form of *it*/**it's**—contraction of *it is*

>The cat licked its fur.

>It's too bad you have to go.

lose—to misplace or come to be without/**loose**—to be free from restraint

>Don't lose your keys.

>He tripped over his loose shoelace.

passed—went by/**past**—an earlier time; beyond

>We passed like ships in the night.

>That's all in the past.

>She walked past without saying a word.

personal—private, intimate/**personnel**—employees

>That happens to be my personal business.

>He was hired by the personnel office.

piece—part of a whole/**peace**—opposite of *war*

>Give me a piece of that pie, please.

>We all want peace.

principal—first in rank; the chief or head/**principle**—an accepted rule or belief

>Elmwood School has a new principal.

>Many arguments have been started over a principle.

quiet—making no noise; peaceable/**quite**—completely or entirely

>All's quiet on the street.

>Now I'm quite lost.

sole—only; the bottom of a foot or shoe/**soul**—the spirit

> She was the sole survivor.

> The shoemaker mended the sole of my shoe.

> She had a beautiful soul.

their—ownership/**there**—in that place/**they're**—contraction of *they are*

> Their coats are hanging in the closet.

> Put it over there.

> They're always very friendly.

to—a preposition; part of any infinitive/**too**—also, excessively/**two**—number after *one*

> I'm going to the mountains.

> I'm too tired to talk.

> You should go, too.

> That's too much whipped cream.

> She ate two hot dogs.

who's—contraction of *who is*/**whose**—the possessive case of *who*

> Who's driving with me?

> Whose scarf is this?

your—the possessive case of *you*/**you're**—contraction of *you are*

> I found your notebook.

> You're the boss.

Although these are not, of course, the only homophones—English is riddled with many others—these are the ones you are most likely to encounter.

PRACTICE 1

Underline the correct word in parentheses for each sentence below.

1. You have (access/excess) to many computers.

2. It will have a severe (affect/effect) on my budget.

3. (Its/It's) too late to (altar/alter) my plans.

4. This is my (forth/fourth) trip to New York.

5. I drove (past/passed) her house with my heart pounding.

6. (There/Their/They're) lies the problem.

7. She said that (its/it's) a matter of (principal/principle).

8. Are you (quite/quiet) finished?

9. He gave me a (piece/peace) of his mind.

10. (Whose/Who's) bringing the salad?

PRACTICE 2

Write a sentence for each of the homophones below.

1. principal _____

principle _____

2. capital _____

capitol _____

3. personal _____

personnel _____

4. course _____

coarse _____

5. sole _____

soul _____

Commonly Misspelled Words

Below is a list of words that are commonly misspelled. If you regularly have trouble with any word on this list, include it in your personal spelling list and keep practicing its correct spelling.

LIST OF COMMONLY MISSPELLED WORDS

accidentally

acquaintance

acquire

address

all right (always two words, just like *all wrong*)

already (not to be confused with *all ready*)

answer

anxious

arithmetic

athletics

attendance

awful

awkward

believe (not to be confused with *belief*)

breathe (not to be confused with *breath*)

business

calendar

cemetery

changeable

chief

choose (not to be confused with *chose*)

conscience (not to be confused with *conscious*)

daily

definite

dependent

design

device (not to be confused with *devise*)

disappearance

embarrass

environment

especially

exaggerate	practically
exercise	precede
existence	preferred
familiar	prejudice
fascinate	preparation
foreign	privilege
forty	proceed
fragrant	receive
friend	recognize
government	referred/referring
grammar	relieve (not to be confused with *relief*)
harass	
height	resemblance
hindrance	restaurant
incredible	reverence
independent	ridiculous
interesting	sandwich
irresistible	seize (not to be confused with *size*)
library	
literature	separate
maintenance	several
mathematics	similar
medicine	sincerely
million	succeed
miracle	surprise
miscellaneous	temperature
mischief	than (not to be confused with *then*)
necessary	
neighbor	thorough
noticeable	tragedy
nuisance	truly
occasion	unnecessary
occur/occurrence/occurred	until
offered	usually
parallel	vegetable
peculiar	visitor
politics	weird
possess	writing

USAGE MONITOR

Don't worry about spelling the words listed below because they don't actually exist. They are instead corrupted substitutes:

- *Thusly* (should be *thus*)
- *Towards* (should be *toward*)
- *Should of* or *could of* (should be *should have* or *could have*)
- *Anyways* or *anywheres* (should be *anyway* or *anywhere*)

PRACTICE 3

Each of the following sentences contains a misspelled word from the list above. Write the correct version in the blank provided.

Example: Their *existance* was in doubt. <u>existence</u>

1. They met each other accidentaly. _____

2. My strong point is athaletics. _____

3. It was not easy to chose between them. _____

4. She can be very changable. _____

5. On this particular issue, his viewpoint was wierd. _____

6. He has his own upholstery bisness. _____

7. I'm so dependant on her. _____

8. Maintenence said the problem was with the water heater.
_____

9. Mathmatics has always been my worst subject. _____

10. It was not necessery to do more. _____

PRACTICE 4

Circle the correctly spelled word in each of the following word pairs.

1. miscellanous/miscellaneous

2. neighbor/naighbor

3. embarrass/embarress

4. conscience/conscence

5. ocasion/occasion

6. occurence/occurrence

7. poletics/politics

8. vegatable/vegetable

9. preparation/preperation

10. tragidy/tragedy

Error 20 Review

The paragraph that follows contains 20 of the spelling errors mentioned in this section. Correct each error.

When I was in grammer school, I made freinds with a foriegn exchange student. His name was Adam, and he was an intaresting kid. He came from England, and was very independant even though he was only eight years old. Early in our acquaintence, we decided to swap accents. So on a dayly basis, we would sit on the playground and try to talk like each other. I was from the South and had a southern accent, while he spoke like a Londoner, which I found irresestible. But much to our suprise, we found that we couldn't do it. Its very hard to capture another person's accent. Trying to do it makes you sound rediculous, or piculiar, to say the least. The other kids used to tease us, which embarassed us. It was hard enough all-ready for Adam to get adjusted without the nuisence of being teased for the way he sounded. We decided to stop the silly buseness of switching accents and just be ourselves. Many years later, on a social ocasion, I met Adam again. By then, we were in our mid-20s, and he had remained in Atlanta. We talked about how the other kids used to harrass us and laughed about it. Not until later did I recanize a funny fact: Adam had ackwired a southern accent and now spoke exactly as I did!

_____

_____

_____

_____

_____

_____

_____

_____

_____

_____

To check your progress in meeting this chapter's objectives, log in to **www.mywritinglab.com,** go to the **Study Plan** tab, click on **The 20 Most Common Sentence Errors** and choose **Easily Confused Words** from the list of subtopics. Read and view the resources in the **Review Materials** section, and then complete the **Recall, Apply,** and **Write** sets in the **Activities** section.

INDEX